Erika and the Skeleton Staff

Written by
Hazel Walshaw

Illustrated by
Ruxandra Șerbănoiu

A catalogue record for this book is available from the British Library

ISBN 978-1-9163087-8-7

First printed 2020
This edition 2025

For more information on the author visit:
www.hazelwalshaw.co.uk
www.facebook.com/hazelwalshawauthor

Thank you to Roisin Heycock and Laura Wilkinson for their editing skills.

For Mackenzie, Morgan and Quinn
The Musketeers of Chaos!

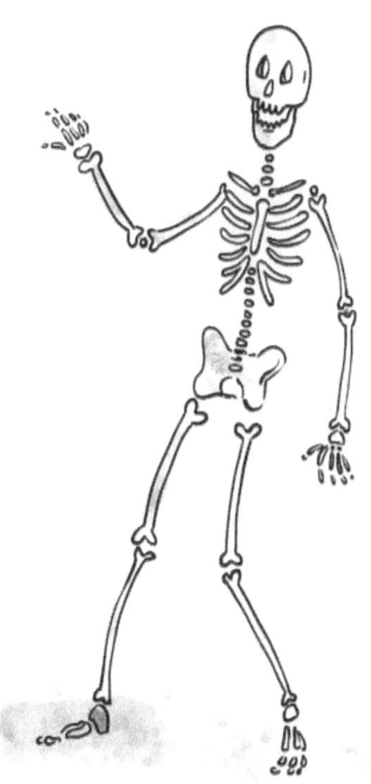

Forward by the author

It's been five years since I first published Erika and the Skeleton Staff.

I was inspired to write it after all the snow we had in 2018 and I got thinking about what if the skeleton staff at school, to keep it open, were real skeletons? What would a snow day be like with them in charge? Would it be scary? What mischief would happen? And a book which starts with mystery, intrigue, and a few scares, became a funny, calamity-packed story as Erika and her friends help out the new 'teachers'.

This was such a fun book to write, and I've loved the responses I've had from children and parents, from across the world, who have read it over that time. A few children even took this book to school on World Book Day and dressed as a skeleton from the book! I feel honoured that my book has made an impression on them so much. It must be something all children's authors want—to see their book being a favourite.

I was lucky to find an amazing illustrator, Ruxandra, who created all the artwork, including the cover. My book would not be the same without her artistic skills. She captured the words into pictures perfectly, and I am exceedingly grateful for her talent.

I should also thank my husband, Neil, and the musketeers of chaos (my boys) for giving me the time to write and inspiring the stories within me.

I have plans to make a sequel—I know it's been a long time coming, but I'm hoping another Erika book, including the hapless skeletons, will make an appearance in late 2025. But don't hold me to that.

Keep reading and imagining... and read on to find out what a skeleton has with his hot chocolate...

Much Love,
Hazel x

Prologue

In the darkness, there was a strange rattling sound followed by a scraping sound. Then a sound of something, or somethings, rolling gently across a stone floor. The sounds could have been mistaken for sticks being gathered into a pile, but they weren't sticks.

Something, or somethings, in the darkness, could sense a change in the air like a static charge. It was coming. After all these years of waiting it would soon be time. They had work to do before it came.

If you had been there, listening to these strange sounds, sounds that shouldn't be coming from a dark basement, you might have heard a hollow, clunking noise, followed by scraping, followed by...an electric screwdriver? And what was that squeaky sound? Something being polished with a cloth? You would have wondered what was going on. Would you stay to find out?

Well, would you?

Chapter 1
Snow Days

My name is Erika, I'm ten years old and I love space, ghost stories and snow. It was a gloomy Sunday evening in the winter. I was sat in the dark of the bedroom with a blanket over my head and a torch lighting up my face from below. I was trying to tell my six-year-old brother, Frank, a ghost story.

"There had been stories told through the years, from Year Six to Reception, of Snow Days!" I spoke in a low tone.

"People say that when school wasn't quite closed, many teachers couldn't get to school from the nearby towns and villages. Half the children stayed home as well. There was talk of something else too..." I paused for dramatic effect."*A skeleton staff!*"

"A what?" Frank looked up from playing his console game, *Cheese-Opolis,* where you build cities out of different types of cheese.

"A skeleton staff," I repeated, annoyed that Frank was interrupting.

"What's a skeleton staff?" he asked, turning back to his game to add blocks of cheddar to make a wall.

"Teachers who are skeletons," I said. "Obvs. Do you want to hear this story or not?"

Mum came into the room and flicked the light on.

"Mum!" Frank and I said in unison.

"We like it dark," Frank added.

She was wearing her usual dress of trainers, leggings and sweatbands, and carrying her gym bag.

"You do have quite the imagination, Erika." She smiled and rubbed my head vigorously.

I didn't mind as much since I had my hair cut short. I didn't want it short, but my mum is useless at hairstyles other than ponytails. High ones, low ones, or side ones, she can tie perfectly. But when she once attempted a French plait, it looked like a blind granny had tried to knit a hat made of hair. Mum was rather relieved when I suggested getting it cut short.

"I'm just off to *Kazoorobics*," she said, waving her Kazoo to make the point.

"Have you remembered your earplugs, Mum?" I asked. She forgot

them last week and twenty-five ladies doing aerobics while blowing Kazoos is quite loud. She was deaf the following day.

"Yes," Mum replied, patting her bag, "Dad's in charge while I'm out."

Me and Frank both let out a laugh. Dad was usually on his phone sorting out a work crisis so just left us to it when

Mum was out.

"Might as well say the dog is in charge," I muttered to Frank after Mum turned the light off and left the room.

"I heard that!" she called back. "Bedtime at eight."

Our dog is called *Wooky*. She's a three-legged, fur-shedding, cuddle monster. She spends most of her time either splayed across Mum's yoga mat, on the TV remote, or across the front doorstep - in any awkward position really.

"I wish we could have snow," I sighed, flashing the torch on and off to make shadows on the wall with my hands. "It would be fun to have skeleton teachers."

I am in year six of St. Winithorpe's Primary School and never in my time at that school has there been a snow day. I live in a small town where snow is rare, or at least doesn't last long enough to affect the school. For so many winters, we would watch the news on TV and see the images of children tobogganing and building snowmen. On the local radio, the presenters would cheerily read out a list of closed schools, but ours was never mentioned. Not once.

We would get flurries of snow, a sprinkling of snow if we were lucky, but no actual proper winter wonderland snow. I can imagine what a snow day would be like though. Normal lessons are cancelled. There is singing in the school hall, hot chocolate instead of milk and we can play games and have snowball fights in the playground. And, of course, find out if the stories of skeletons were true.

Chapter 2
What's That?

St. Winithorpe's Primary school was built over one hundred years ago. It is cold and draughty in the winter and boiling hot in the summer. There is only a small two-week window in the spring and autumn when the temperature is bearable.

It has a central courtyard-style playground and a small playing field across the road for P.E. and sports day. OFSTED had rated it as "Surprisingly Adequate". Children came from quite a distance to go to it instead of to the other one, rated "Better than not going to school".

I got to school early on Monday, like I usually did, to help our teacher,

Mrs Willis, set up. I'm the helpful sort.

"Ah, excellent, Erika," Mrs Willis said when she saw me. "Can you go to the Year Five classroom, please? There is a box of books on the Solar System that Mr McDainty has left out for us."

"Ooh! I love space! I want to be an astrophysicist when I grow up!"

"An excellent career choice, Erika," Mrs Willis replied. "However, you'll need to stop daydreaming and concentrate on your maths."

I headed off to the Year Five classroom in the old part of the school. The school was once a small building comprising of a hall, a couple of classrooms and a corridor. It was built in the early 1900s, with a whole new building added on in the 1960s. So, even the new bit is now old, but it is still called the old or new part of the school.

The old bit has a creepy feel to it. There is a feeling of history with the initials of hundreds of previous school children etched into the woodwork. There was a small locked door along the corridor that no one had opened in years as far as I could tell. It rattled as I walked past.

I could see the Year Five teacher, Mr McDainty, sat in the classroom through the glass window in the door. He was looking towards the left-hand side of the room and appeared to be talking to someone. I knocked at the door and waited.

"Enter," Mr McDainty said after a short pause.

He was facing the door as I enter and coughed.

"I've come to collect some books,

Sir," I said. Mr McDainty was an old-
fashioned teacher and still preferred to
be called Sir.

"They're by the door, Erika."

Mr McDainty took his round
glasses off and gave them a clean
before putting them back on.

"Don't let me hold you up." He
coughed a few more times.

I picked the box up and glanced
around the classroom before
leaving.

There wasn't anyone else in the room, so I didn't know who Mr McDainty was talking to, though I may have imagined that. As I turned to shut the door behind me, I caught sight of a dark shadow in the corner of the room. Then the heavy door swung shut and whatever I thought I saw was out of sight.

What had I seen?
There was something, but what was it?

I couldn't go back in. I'd have to wait and sneak a peek another time.
A chill passed through me as I walked by the small door in the corridor, which gave a

louder rattle, making me jump. I broke into a run back to my classroom with the box of books, despite the *No Running in the Corridor* rule.

Chapter 3
The News Report

Dad got home from work more excited than usual and rushed to put the TV on – yep the news. But, this time it actually was exciting. The news presenter was finishing up one of those local interest stories about cats or squirrels or something and was announcing the weather:

"Now let's go over to Gloria and see what the weather has in store for us over the next couple of days. Gloria?"

Gloria appeared on screen - far too much make- up for 6.30 pm if you ask me - and flashed her bright white smile.

"Thanks, Michael," Gloria said

with her silky-smooth voice. "Well, it's going to be getting colder this week as a low front swoops in from the east," Gloria swooped her arms and body from right to left on the screen, "in the early hours of Wednesday morning, bringing with it sleet and snow. Some areas could be expected to see up to ten inches of snow, so do remember to wrap up warm."

She then added, creepily: "It will chill you to the bone."

"Thank you for the warning, Gloria," Michael replied after a pause. Mum switched the TV off.

Me and Frank let out a cheer so loud it could be heard at the end of the road. **_Snow!_** Actual snow. On a school day!

Frank started doing the *cheese*

string dance from his *Cheese-Opolis* game. This caused the dog to start barking. For about five minutes, there was quite a rumpus going on in the living room. Dad took to social media to check local travel plans and bus contingency options, and to see if there were gritters available.

"Mum, is it true that they have skeletons in school during snow days?" Frank asked.

Mum laughed, "Have you been listening to Erika's stories again? Don't let her imagination frighten you, it's just an expression for a small number of staff. I know, I'll pull you both to school on a sledge. We should have one in the shed somewhere." Mum left the room.

"Actual skeletons," I said.
Frank looked at me to see if I was joking or not.

"That's what I've heard," I said.

I couldn't wait to get to school the next day to discuss what was going to happen on Wednesday.

As I laid in bed that evening, the wind was blowing and making the windows rattle. I remembered the rattling door at school and the strange thing I saw, or thought I saw, in the classroom. I shivered and pulled the duvet over my head. I had strange dreams of skeletons rattling at my door that night.

Chapter 4
Snow Day T Minus 1 Day

At school on Tuesday, I met up with my friends, Aisha, Danny, and Arthur to discuss the weather report.

"Did you see the news?" I excitedly asked as soon as I saw them.

"Yeah. Snow! Can't believe it!" Danny said.

"My dad said I could stay home tomorrow," Aisha said, smiling at the thought of a day off.

"No, you can't, Aisha," I said. "It's a snow day. There could be a skeleton staff!"

Arthur snorted. "Skeleton staff? What's that?"

"Mum says it's a small number of teachers, but the stories say that it is actual skeletons," I said.

"What stories? Don't be daft," Danny retorted.

"Humph," I folded my arms. "We'll see."

During the assembly that morning, the headteacher, Mrs Squires, announced what I already knew.

"There is snow forecast for tomorrow, children," she said in her deep calming voice.

One hundred and fifty children all started chattering at once in excitement. It took a few minutes to get them all settled down and quiet again. In the end, it was the reception teacher who restored order by getting all the children to put their fingers on their lips.

"Thank you, Miss Sweet. Now,

where were we...ah yes. Snow." Mrs Squires started pacing back and forth. She had a habit of doing that.

"It has been so long since there was snow, I had to look up the procedure in the school's *'Procedures, Policies, and Emerging Planet Guide'.*"

It's possible she meant *Emergency Planning*, but no one corrected her. She waved the dusty guide at us. The dust made her cough and settled on her hair, turning it grey. It was very dusty.

"Now we are obligated to keep the school open where possible for any children who are local and are able to make it in." There was a disappointed groan from the local children who were hoping for a day off.

"Yay," I said under my breath to Aisha. Finally.

"Mr McDainty and Miss Bellows

live within walking distance and will be here along with," she paused to examine a sheet of paper in her hand. "A couple of former teachers, who have kindly offered to help. So, there will be a skeleton staff to watch over you as I do appreciate some of your parents still have to work."

I turned to Danny triumphantly.

"That doesn't mean they're real

skeletons," he whispered.

At the mention of skeleton staff, I noticed that Mr McDainty and Miss Bellows shared a look with each other.

A few children raised their hands.

"Yes, Isabelle?" asked Mrs Squires

"How tall are the skeletons looking after us? Are they scary?" Isabelle asked.

The headteacher, surprised, said

reassuringly, "It's just an expression. Skeleton staff means only a few teachers so the school is kept open."

"See," Danny said.

Again, I noticed the quick glances between Mr McDainty and Miss Bellows. Mr McDainty coughed again.

Now, a bit of information on these two teachers. Both have been at this school the whole time I have been here and I'm pretty sure they taught some of our parents as well. So, they're like ancient or something. Not overly keen on change, but they do their best.

Mr McDainty is a stickler for formality, rules and shiny shoes. Never missed a day of school as far as I remember. Miss Bellows is a very tiny lady. Softly spoken and kind. Known to hand out sweets and hair ribbons when the mood took her. We'd do anything for Miss Bellows.

The questions came in thick and fast:

"Can we build a snowman?"
"Can we have a snowball fight?"
"Will there be hot chocolate?"
"Can we sing songs from *Freezing?*"

Mrs Squires decided it was a good time to finish and sent us back to our classrooms for our teachers to deal with.

"Did you notice the looks Mr McDainty and Miss Bellows were giving each other during assembly?" I asked Aisha.

"No," she said. "What were they doing?"

"It was when Mrs Squires mentioned the skeleton staff. They looked...I don't know...weird. Like they knew something the headteacher didn't."

"It's your imagination, Erika," said Aisha.

"Well, they have been at this school since dinosaurs roamed the earth," piped up Danny.

"My brother's, cousin's, best friend's dad said they've been here since the school was built," said Arthur. Arthur always knew someone who knew someone who had an answer for everything.

"That would make them about..." Aisha shut her eyes while doing a mental calculation, "one hundred and twenty years old," she said after only a short pause. Maths is her speciality.

"Only passing on what I heard," Arthur said.

Back at the classroom, Mrs Willis got us settled down and doing maths until lunchtime. I wasn't really concentrating. I kept thinking about those looks between Mr McDainty and Miss Bellows when skeleton staff were mentioned. And also, that strange feeling I got when I was in the Year Five classroom yesterday. Which also meant I was having my own questions in my head:

If there were real skeletons, where do they live when it's not snowing? Do they need to be unpacked? Do they arrive on a bus? Are they airdropped in? No, that would be silly. They would break apart on impact.

What was the something, I couldn't quite put my finger on, in Mr McDainty's classroom? What had I seen? I shook my head and tried to get on with fractions. I looked across at Aisha. She had already finished.

My curiosity was starting to get the better of me. I felt that a wander around the school at lunchtime would be in order. I was sure something was not quite right. I was about to be proven correct.

Chapter 5
Curiosity

When the bell for lunch rang, I decided to stay back in the classroom, pretending to finish my maths. Mrs Willis seemed keen for me to leave, but she sighed, "Don't hang around too long and go get your lunch," then headed out the door.

Aisha, Danny, and Arthur were waiting for me when I left the classroom.

"What you doing?" asked Aisha.

"I'm going to have a look in the Year Five classroom. I just feel that something isn't quite right," I replied.

Arthur made a spooky noise and wriggled his fingers at me, "Do do do do, do do do do."

"I had a strange feeling yesterday when I was picking up books," I ignored him. "I thought I saw something. Are you going to come and check it out with me?"

"Sure," said Danny. "It's fish pie and cabbage for lunch. I looked in the kitchen earlier and it was grey. I'm not eating grey food."

We headed down the corridor towards the old part of the school. We had to pass the staff room so we looked down the corridor to check the coast was clear and then ducked past the staff room door, through the hall and into the short corridor with the two classrooms on the other side.

These classrooms were the domain of Mr McDainty, who teaches Year Five, and Miss Bellows who teaches Year One.

It seemed strange that those year classrooms were next to each other. But that's the years they teach and that was where they always taught them. It's how it had always been. Only now it seem odd.

As we approached the classroom Danny peeked through the window in the door to check the room was empty. He gave a convoluted signal of gestures. When we all looked at him and shrug, he sighed, "Yes, it's empty. Come on!"

We entered the classroom and stood in a small group by the door. We had this classroom last year, so it was familiar. Yet...yet, there was something different. We looked about and then we all found our eyes drawn to the same part of the classroom. We stood stock-still.

We were not alone.

Chapter 6
Be Brave

In the corner stood a sinister, tall object covered in a black cloth. It definitely hadn't been there when we were in Year Five. It was new.

"So, *this* is what I saw when I was here yesterday," I said. "I knew I'd seen something." I was mildly pleased to be proven right.

The object was about the same height as a person. It was a similar width as well. I took Arthur's hand and told him to be brave. He rolled his eyes at me, but I noticed he didn't let go. So, I dropped his hand and wiped my hand on my jumper.

We inched toward the corner of the room; our eyes glued to the tall, person-sized, cloth-covered object. It seemed to be pulling us towards it. The air around the object had a strong, almost overpowering smell, a bit like furniture polish. It made me cough and I felt my hair stand on end as we got up close.

"I'm going to lift the cloth and see what it is," I said bravely, though I wasn't feeling brave and my heart was pounding.

"What do you think it is, Erika?" asked Aisha. I didn't say anything. I had my suspicions, I hoped it was just my overactive imagination.

I moved my hand towards the cloth and took hold of the hem. I counted to five and then slowly lifted

the cloth up. We were all holding our
breaths. As the cloth raised, we caught
sight of something white,
lots of little white things, all
joined together to form a... a...

skeleton foot!

"**Argh!**"

I dropped the cloth and jumped back, falling into Danny and knocking him over. The spell over us was broken and we scrambled to our feet and rushed towards the door. Out in the corridor, we all stopped to catch our breaths.

"What was that?" wailed Danny, pointing towards the classroom door.

"I had my eyes shut," said Aisha, shaking her head, "I saw nothing."

"It was a skeleton," I said in disbelief. "They're here ready for tomorrow."

We stood in silence for a few moments taking the situation in. We didn't notice Mr McDainty standing in the doorway to the hall.

"What are you four doing here?" he asked.

We all jumped at his voice, but we were still too spooked to reply.

"Shouldn't you be at lunch?"

We were silently ushered towards the dining room to see what was left. The grey fish pie and cabbage was not appealing but there was sponge and custard if we had it first.

And we were prepared to put up with any horrible food for sponge and custard.

Chapter 7
Preparations

The afternoon passed without incident, learning about the Solar System. Though it was my favourite topic, I found it hard to concentrate. I had visions of skeletons taking over the school. Soon the going home bell rang out. I raced home, dragging Frank along, as there were preparations to make. If skeletons were going to be terrorising the school, I was going to be ready to be the hero and bring them down.

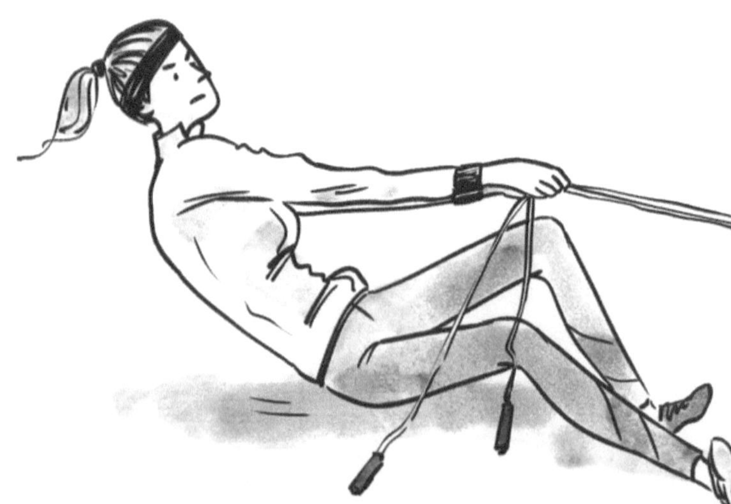

When I got home my mum was in her aerobic gear again having a tug of war with the dog. It looked like quite a workout. The dog had hold of her skipping rope and was growling. Mum was trying to get her to open her mouth with a dog treat but Wooky was refusing to let go.

I went into the kitchen to get a drink. When I got back into the sitting room, my mum was winding the skipping rope back up, having finally got it back from the dog.

"How was school Erika?" asked Mum.

"Fine," I replied.

"What did you do today?" she asked hopefully.

"Nothing," I said.

"What was for lunch?" she tried again.

"Don't remember."

"It was only two hours ago! Oh, never mind." She gave up interrogating me about my day and left the room. Ten seconds later, I heard her shout "Get off my Yoga Mat, stupid dog!" and I could hear her trying to shift our large dog off it.

After tea, in my bedroom, I got out some paper and felt tip pens and drew a map of the school. I marked on the location of the skeleton in the Year Five classroom. I then marked on potential hiding places and ambush points between my classroom, the hall and the classroom with the skeleton in. I didn't know how many teachers would be in school tomorrow, but if there was only one skeleton, the odds were still in our favour.

I rolled up the map and put it in my school bag. Then I went into Frank's room and we sat and stared at the sky until bedtime, waiting for the snow.

Chapter 8
Snow! And More Snow!

It did snow during the night. A lot. Well, for a town that never gets snow the few inches we got were like the North Pole to me and Frank. Wooky was bounding around the garden and barking at everything. Frank was singing his favourite song, 'Baby Poo poo poo poo-poo', to include the word 'snow' instead of 'poo'. This didn't stop it being annoying. Dad was on the phone to the planning department. I could hear him saying, "...thawed by this evening..." as he glared at Frank and his singing. Then the door to his office closed.

Picture the scene. Mum was dressed for the Winter Olympics and me and Frank looked like knitted Weebles.

Wrapped in multicoloured scarves, hats and gloves we waddled out to the sledge. Mum did a few stretches, and took hold of the rope and pulled.

We were off to school!

As Mum's boots crunched through the new snow, I was feeling a mix of fear and excitement. Part of me wished we were staying home, safe and warm, and not being pulled to possible (or indeed certain) doom. But I wouldn't get the chance to experience a snow day in school again.

And that skeleton. I had to find out what was going on and be ready to protect my friends and Frank.

I felt like I was the only one who knew what was in store.

Frank started asking about skeletons again, but Mum pretended not to hear. Once we reached the school gates, we dismounted. Mum gave us both a kiss and a cheery goodbye and then headed back home with the sledge. We turned to face the school.

As we walked up to the main entrance, I happened to glance through the window of the classroom next door to ours. Something I saw sent a wave of fear running through me.

In the corner of the Year Four classroom, I had just seen a tall white figure.

Chapter 9
Uh-Oh!

As there were few children at school today, everyone was to go straight to the hall.

I decided to have a look in the Year Four classroom before going to the hall. I gave my friends the slip as I needed to check if I had really seen another skeleton.

As I opened the door, my heart was pounding in my chest. I looked over to the corner of the room and there it was. The skeleton was standing in the corner. There was something about it. There was an energy in the room. As I looked at it, it seemed to change from a collection of bones to something that was...alive.

I realised too late I had let go of the door and it shut with a loud clunk behind me. I waited, not daring to move or breathe. I kept my eyes on the skeleton. Was this the same one we saw yesterday? Or was this a different one? This one appeared taller.

Then it moved its head...In my direction. Could it see me?

The limbs of the skeleton started to jiggle about, and its head tilted from side to side in a strange wobbly way. Something was happening to it.

And then it jerked and started moving, slowly in my direction. It had a limp. At first, I was paralysed with fear and then, as it got nearer, I regained control of my legs and I knew I had to take action. And that action was to get out of there as quickly as possible.

I dived back into my classroom and looked for a potential weapon to defend myself. Panicked, I grabbed the nearest thing to hand, a copy of the concise English Dictionary. I was not sure if I would bamboozle it with large words or throw the book at its skull. I waited behind the door and peered through the window, clutching the book to my chest for comfort.

The Year Four classroom door opened, and the skeleton walked out of the classroom. It turned its head to look up and down the corridor and then it turned away from where I was hiding and moved down the corridor. I could hear the uneven clip-clop sound as the skeleton limped away. As the sound faded, I realised that it was heading to

the hall where everyone was gathered,
waiting for the big announcement.

I must get to it before it got
them. I had to be a hero. I opened the
door and looked down the corridor
before following the skeleton.

As I was getting close to it and ready to strike with my dictionary. the staff room door opened, just in front of the skeleton. Miss Bellows came out into the corridor. I lowered the book and stopped.

"Phew!" I thought, she would turn and see the skeleton and sort it all out and all would be well.

She did turn. She lifted her head to look up at the skeleton that towered over her. She seemed to take seeing a six-foot skeleton extremely well. She then walked to the hall doors, opened them, and smiling, let the skeleton walk right in!

Uh-oh...this was bad. **Really bad.** The teachers were in on the whole thing! We were going to get eaten by skeletons. Well, probably not eaten as we could climb out through the ribcage, couldn't we? Ah, I was getting distracted. What to do now?

"Erika, are you joining us?" Miss Bellows turned to me, holding open the door.

I froze to the spot unsure of my next move. Maybe Miss Bellows was under some sort of spell the skeletons had cast over the school? Was I the only one not under it? Could I break it?

I realised I had no choice but to go into the hall and see what was going on.

"Yes, Miss," I replied, slowly walking past her.

"You won't be needing that," She said, holding out her hands for the Dictionary.

"No, Miss."

I handed the book over and entered the hall.

This was really very bad indeed.

Chapter 10
This Is Not What I Expected

The hall was only half-full. I found a space on the floor next to my friends.

Mr McDainty was already standing at the front of the hall with one skeleton. I assumed it was the one we saw yesterday. Miss Bellows walked up the centre of the hall, following the taller, limping skeleton. So, there were two.

"We're doomed," I said looking at the line up at the front of the hall. Two teachers and two skeletons.

Danny was excited and he shook my arm. "Look at that! Skeleton staff!

You're not daft after all."

I wished I was daft, and that this nightmare was not happening.

"So cool," said Arthur.

"No, not cool," I hissed. "It's really bad."

At least my friends didn't appear to be under any spell.

"We must get that looked at, Mr Jenkins," Mr McDainty said.

Who's Mr Jenkins? There were no other teachers here. We sat quietly and the younger children looked a bit scared. We all waited.

"Children," started Miss Bellows. "As you can see, only myself and Mr McDainty could make it to school today, so we have a skeleton staff to watch over you for the day."

So, Mrs Squires and Mum were wrong. The skeleton staff were actual skeletons.

I waited for the order for the skeletons to attack. I glanced at Aisha. She was staring straight ahead, looking confused.

Mr McDainty then said, "Let me introduce our temporary staff to you. We have here the former Mr Jenkins." Mr McDainty turned to the taller skeleton with the limp.

"He had been a teacher here from 1932-1940 when he had to leave to fight in The Second World War. He then taught here again from 1945 until his death in 1953 when he, unfortunately, died falling into a vat of rice pudding."

A few children chuckled but Mr McDainty glared them into silence.

"This is the former Mrs Dean," Miss Bellows said, pointing to the shorter skeleton.

"She was a teacher here when it was an all-girls school for eleven to sixteen-year-olds from 1963 until 1972. She died in a regrettable incident, when a large group of teenagers in platform shoes mowed her down outside the staff room. Someone thought they had seen the tour van of the infamous band *Now Then* outside the school. Fifty screaming girls headed out into the street leaving a flattened Mrs Dean in their wake."

"The former Mr Jenkins will oversee Years Four and Six and the former Mrs Dean will oversee Years Two and Three," said Mr McDainty. "I will cover Year Five as usual and Miss Bellows Year One and Reception."

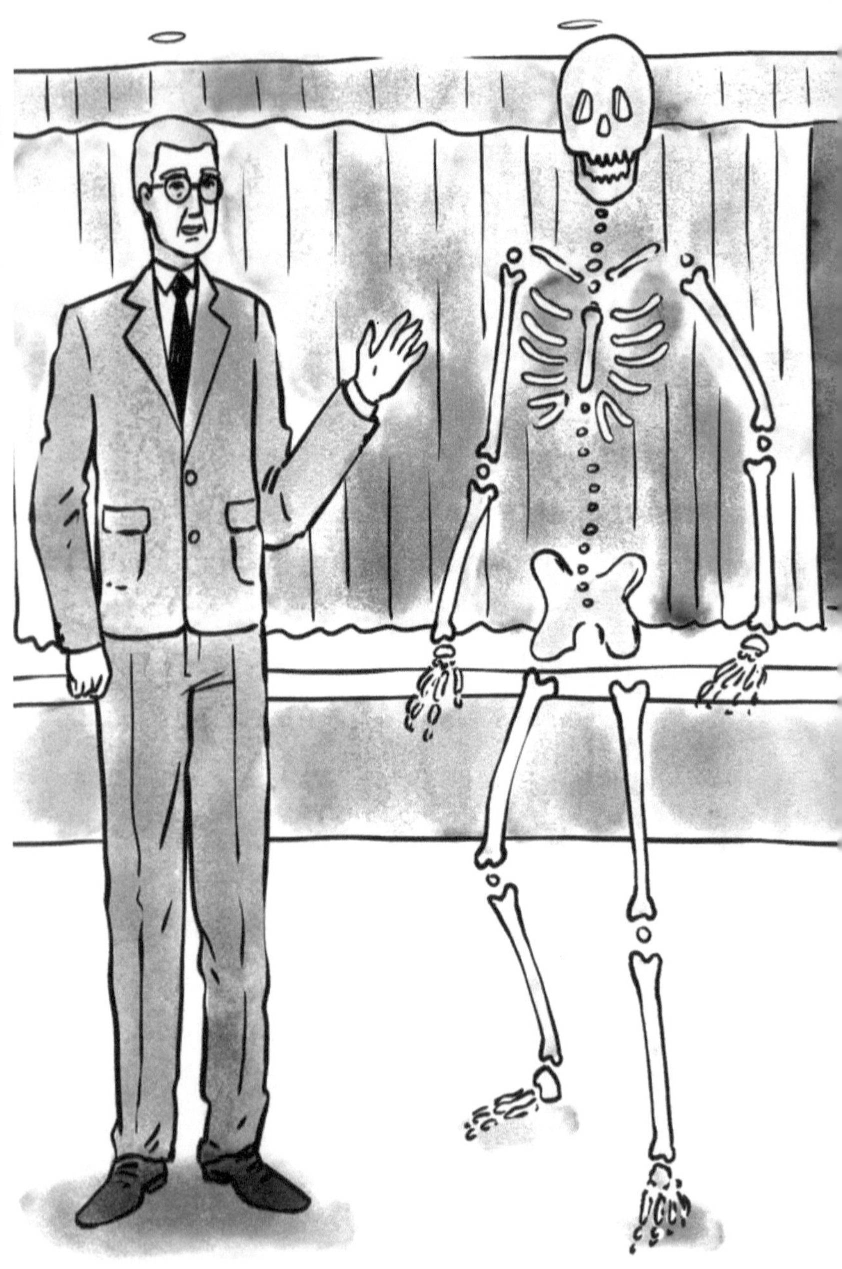

This was not what I expected.

Suddenly, the doors banged open, making us all jump, and a third skeleton came into the hall. This one moved in a jauntier way, swinging its arms and nodding its head. It joined the other two at the front of the hall.

"This is Dave." Mr McDainty sighed and gestured to the third skeleton. There's always a Dave. "He'll be in charge of the catering."
Another pause.
A hand was raised.
"Yes, Jessica?" Mr McDainty asked, knowing full well what was coming.
"How did he die?" She squealed.

Children love a good death story, and everyone leaned forward to get the full details.

"Well ,if you must know..."

I was too busy thinking about the change in events to listen. How maybe today was not going to be full of doom. I wondered why Mr McDainty didn't ever teach other children except Year Five's. When my brain re-joined the assembly, Mr McDainty was finishing up, "...but that was the 90's for you."

A stunned silence followed this.

"What did I miss?" I nudged Aisha.

She turned to look at me open mouthed.

"Wild times," Arthur said shaking his head in disbelief.

Miss Bellows clapped her hands together, bringing all the children out from whatever spell the story of Dave's death had caused. "Right, children, Year

Six to go to the Year Four classroom for today. Years Two and Three in the Year Two classroom and I'll have Year One and Reception with me," Miss Bellows said.

"Year Five, follow me," Mr McDainty said.

Ah, so the skeleton I was going to take out with the dictionary was the former Mr Jenkins. I looked at it. It turned its head and looked at me. At least I think it was looking at me. It felt like it was looking at me, despite it not having any eyes.

We all trooped in lines back to the classroom.

"I'll be over to repair you in ten minutes Mr Jenkins," Mr McDainty added over his shoulder as he led the Year Five students out of the hall.

I wonder how you repair a skeleton?

Chapter 11
How Do You Repair a Skeleton?

It turned out that you need an electric screwdriver, some duct tape, and some wire.

Mr McDainty had the former Mr Jenkins laid out on the carpet in front of the interactive whiteboard. He was using the electric screwdriver and duct tape to try and even out the leg lengths to reduce the limping. The skeleton also pointed out his right arm was a bit loose as well.

"This is what happens when you try to repair yourselves in the dark," Mr McDainty chided his skeletal patient.

A few more screws and some more

lengths of duct tape later and the former Mr Jenkins was repaired.

"Should see you through until home time anyway," Mr McDainty said. He took his tools and tape and headed to the classroom door.

"Or should I say, 'see through you'," he chuckled to himself as he went out.

The former Mr Jenkins shook his head like he had heard that joke quite a few times. If he could have rolled his eyes, he would have done.

The skeleton swung his arms and kicked his legs to check they were in good working order. He turned to the interactive whiteboard. He then looked around and seemed confused.

He made a writing motion with his hand and then turned his palms up as if to say, "where do I write?"

Danny went over to the board and switched it on. The former Mr Jenkins jumped back as the screen lit up and he stared at it wide-eyed. Well, to be honest that was the only way he could look.

"Times have moved on since you were a teacher, Sir," said Aisha politely. "We don't have chalk-boards anymore."

The skeleton gave a gesture to say, "how does this work?" and Arthur came forward. "Me, me! Let me show you." The former My Jenkins nodded.

"Ooh, show him the space stuff we've been looking at," I suggested.

They had some awesome videos of the Solar System, presented by that lovely scientist my mum liked. The one with the soft voice and leather jacket.

"Oh yes!" Arthur replied and he started pressing and swiping at the screen. The former Mr Jenkins seemed intrigued by this and he stepped up to the board and put his bony finger on the screen. He pressed. Nothing happened. He tried swiping. Nothing happened except for a horrible grating sound. He tried a few more times. He took hold of Arthur's hand to examine it, then looked at his own bony fingers. He dropped Arthur's hand and gave a small shrug. Bone doesn't work on a touch screen.

I love science and space. As the planets appeared on the screen, the soothing voice of the scientist described the marvels and wonders of the Solar System. I looked across at the skeleton to see if he also loved it.

He was stood with his mouth open.

"It's jaw-dropping, Sir!" Danny quipped.

We spent an hour or so showing the former Mr Jenkins how the board worked. Under his guidance and gestures, we showed him a lot of our learning. He was especially impressed by the maths programme. Well, I think he

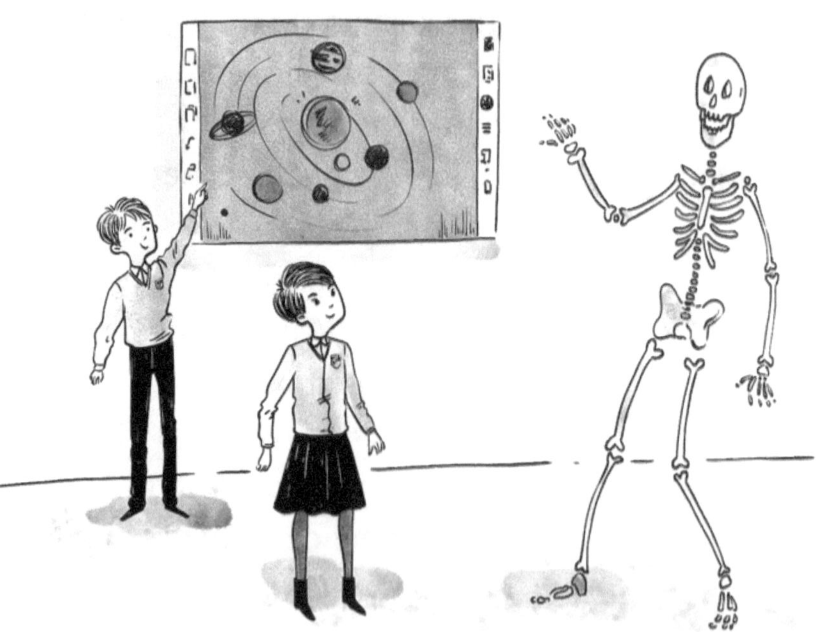

was impressed it was hard to tell.

"Sir!" said Aisha excitedly, "some of the children are outside playing. Can we go outside now?"

The skeleton nodded.

Chapter 12
Can a Skeleton Do the Cheese-String?

We were given rules before we headed out. Miss Bellows had written them down and I read them out loud:

1. No snowballs to the face.
2. No snowballs down the backs of necks or coats.
3. Snow Angels are permitted but no complaining when you are all cold and wet.
4. Snowpeople under 5ft tall are permitted. There should be no gender bias, but neither should they be anatomically correct (what does that mean?).
5. The skeletons are there to watch over you and will report back if there

is any rule-breaking.

A group of Year Two and Three children, including Frank, were already outside. Snowpeople were under construction. The former Mr Jenkins came out the door after us. He seemed a bit hesitant at the top of the steps that led down from the classroom's outside door to the playground. They did look a bit icy in places and bone was quite shiny and...

"Whoa!" exclaimed Danny. "Look at that. He's dancing!"

We all turned to look at the former Mr Jenkins.

He desperately tried to keep his footing and was beginning to flail his arms and legs in all directions. At one point, the hips started jerking from side to side and the arms were moving from side to side in the opposite direction to compensate.

"It's not just any dance," shouted Frank. "It's the *cheese string!*"

This being one of Frank's and, indeed, most of the children's favourite dance - they all joined in and laughed.

Then the Skeleton's moves changed. The arms started circling forward, then back, and the feet were slipping back and forth. They were picking up speed. If he fell, it was going to be spectacular.

It was spectacular.

The former Mr Jenkins had built up momentum with the whirling arms and had managed to propel himself down the steps at terrific speed. He fell forward and went into a cartwheel.

The momentum kept him going all the way across the playground. Children dived face-first into the snow out of the path of the pin-wheeling, six-foot, bony skeleton. He was heading straight towards the snowman (sorry snow*person*) the children had just finished.

FLUMP!

The impact was impressive.

The repair work performed on the skeleton had come loose during the arm flailing. The screw holding the right arm on flew out and his bony arm followed suit.

The skeleton pulled himself free of
the remains of the snowperson and looked
around for his arm. It was handed to him
by a little girl from Year Two.

The skeleton took it and skidded
back across the playground with as much
dignity as a skeleton who, quite frankly,
had made a complete fool of himself, could
muster. When he reached the steps, it
was almost pitiful watching him try to
climb them.

In the end, the undignified retreat

was made even more undignified by the former Mr Jenkins getting his foot trapped in the door as it swung shut behind him.

"What a numskull," Danny said. "Numb. Skull?" he repeated in case we hadn't heard.

He bent down to pick up some snow.

"Snowball fight!" he shouted, throwing a snowball straight into Arthur's face.

As he turned to run, I was ready. I grabbed hold of Danny's coat and...

"Eek!"

...a handful of snow went straight down the back of Danny's neck.

Chapter 13
What Does a Skeleton Have With His Hot Chocolate?

All the snow in the playground had been turned into an army of snowpeople. So, we trooped inside for hot chocolate.

Miss Bellows was already in the dining room with the younger children. There were only about five who had come in. There was a long table set up with an urn and plastic cups.

Skeleton Dave was at the urn with a ladle and was serving the hot chocolate into the cups. There was a radio on in the kitchen behind and Dave was jigging to the music, making box shapes with his hands in between ladling hot chocolate into cups.

At one point, he lifted his arms high to wave them in the air.

Unfortunately, he was still holding a full ladle.

The hot chocolate went all over his head and dripped through his body and onto the floor, forming a chocolate puddle.

"What does a skeleton have with his hot chocolate?" piped up Danny, looking amused.

"I don't know," said Arthur. "What does a skeleton have with his hot chocolate?"

"A mop!" Danny doubled up with laughter and slapped his thigh at his own joke.

Seriously his skeleton jokes were getting out of hand.

Miss Bellows came over to where we were sitting.

"While I have you all here, I just need to tell you that Mrs Squires does not know about our little arrangement here," she said in a quiet voice.

"Who does she think is working today?" I asked.

"She does know a Mr Jenkins and a Mrs Dean, who are former teachers, are here today," she said. "She just doesn't know that they are, well, skeletons."

"So, you need us to keep a secret from the headteacher?" Danny asked.

"Yes, and from your parents too," she said. "If it came out that skeletons were looking after children in the school then it would not be good for Mr McDainty or myself."

"You can count on us," Arthur said.

"Thank you. Right, back to your classrooms while I get Dave to clean up this mess before lunch."

Miss Bellows glided away to speak to Skeleton Dave before rounding up her diminished class.

I heard the distant sound of a telephone ringing in the school office. No one was there to answer it. Which was unfortunate.

Chapter 14
A Cruel Joke

We spent the time up until lunch reading or drawing in our classroom. At lunchtime, when the bell rang, we lined up and followed the former Mr Jenkins to the dining room. His limp had returned, and he kept clip-clopping off to the left and having to straighten up again.

There were only about 50 children in today. Those of us who had packed lunches sat at a table by the windows overlooking the empty, snow-covered car park.

Skeleton Dave was in charge of dinner. He was wearing an apron and chefs hat, and hanging from his ribs were various utensils for serving up. He had a fish slice, a ladle, a couple of large spoons and a spatula dangling from his ribs. They were clanging together as he moved. Which he did a lot.

"What are they having?" asked Frank loudly, craning his neck to see.

"Hotdogs and beans, lucky things," Danny said, taking the top off his sandwich, removing the greenery and replacing the bread.

"Shift up," Arthur said, sliding in with his plate. "I've been informed there is enough pudding for everyone to have."

"What's for pudding?" I asked.

"Don't know. Miss Bellows said Dave was being secretive about it," said Arthur.

Danny eyed up Arthur's plate of hotdogs and beans, then looked at his own limp sandwich. He glanced across at Dave and the hotdogs and made a decision. He shoved the sandwich back into his lunchbox and got up.

He sat back down a minute later with his plate, looking all smug.

"Bone appetite!" he announced as he bit into his hotdog.

"Danny!" we groaned in unison.

Ten minutes later, Dave appeared carrying a large metal pan, which the remaining utensil clanked against as he walked. He put it down on the serving table, removed the ladle from his rib and went to get bowls and spoons.

"Mmm. What's that smell?" asked Aisha.

"Smells creamy," I said.

Suddenly, there was a bit of commotion. The former Mr Jenkins was shaking his fist at Dave and limping away to the furthest corner of the room.

"Oh, Dave!" boomed Mr McDainty. "You know Mr Jenkins has a fear of rice pudding!"

Dave made a gesture as if to say,

"I didn't know," and then shrugged.

"No respect, that man...er... skeleton," Mr McDainty said to Miss Bellows.

"True," she replied. "Still. I do love rice pudding," she added, holding out her bowl to Dave who was ready with his ladle.

We all formed a line for pudding. I looked at the former Mr Jenkins, cowering in a corner.

"Well, you can't blame him, really. What a way to die," I said, holding out my bowl to Dave. "Death by rice pudding."

"Yep, he met a sticky end," Danny said.

While we were eating our pudding, I glanced into the car park. There was now a car parked in it. It was Mrs Squires' car. *And she was getting out of it.*

Chapter 15
Headteacher on the Loose!

"Miss Bellows?" I ran over to where her and Mr McDainty were sitting. "We have a problem. Mrs Squires is here!"

Miss Bellows and Mr McDainty jumped to their feet.

"Dave! Hide in the kitchen!" Mr McDainty ordered. "And where's Mrs Dean?"

"I can see her in the playground, Sir!" called Danny from the far window.

"Right, Danny and Arthur, go find her and hide her somewhere."

"Erika, do something with Mr Jenkins," said Miss Bellows, "I'll greet Mrs Squires and try to keep her busy."

Miss Bellows left to slow the

advance of Mrs Squires. Mr McDainty headed the other way to his classroom. Me and Aisha went over to the former Mr Jenkins.

"Mr Jenkins, Sir, you need to get off the floor now. You need to hide," I said. He didn't move. We both pulled on an arm each to try and get him off the floor. His right arm came off in my hands.

"Sorry, Mr Jenkins," I said, placing his arm on the nearest table.

He got off the floor but only made it as far as a chair before slumping down on it.

"What do we do?" asked Aisha.

I thought for a moment. "Maybe we can dress him up? Are there any coats and hats about?"

"In lost property? But probably all too small. We could borrow Mr McDainty's coat? That would fit."

"Great idea. You watch out for Mrs Squires and I'll get the coat."

I ignored the *No running in the corridor* rule for the second time that week and sprinted to the Year Five classroom.

"Mr McDainty, can we borrow your coat to disguise Mr Jenkins? We can't get him to...Mr McDainty?"

"Call me Mr Jenkins, Erika," said Mr McDainty in a...what was that? A Scottish accent? And what was he wearing?

Mr McDainty had on a brightly coloured Christmas sweater. It had a reindeer on it with bells on the antlers. He was sat behind his desk and was putting a wig on with the help of a couple of Year Five children.

"This scenario is not unexpected, Erika. This happened once during the big snow of '93. We made sure we would be prepared if it happened again." His bells jingled gently.

I left the classroom with Mr McDainty's coat and hat. Miss Bellows was leading Mrs Squires across the hall when I got there.

"Everything alright, Erika?" asked Miss Bellows with a wink.

"Yes. Good afternoon, Mrs Squires," I said as I kept moving.

In the dining hall, Aisha was hopping around nervously.

"Mrs Squires almost came in here!" she said. "But Frank distracted her outside the door, singing that song he sings all the time,"

"Not the Baby Poo one??" I said, alarmed at the thought of my brother singing a song about poo to the headteacher."

"No, the other one."

That was a relief. Mrs Squires would have had that song in her head for days. We tried putting Mr Jenkins in the coat and hat. It was quite difficult as he wasn't co-operating. Frank flung the door open making us jump.

"Mrs Squires is coming!"

We could hear her footsteps getting nearer. There was no time to do anything but give the skeleton a shove. He fell under the table and I dropped the coat over the top of him.

Aisha rushed forward and started asking Mrs Squires about maths in the hope of distracting her from the heap of skeleton and coat on the floor. I used my foot to push him further under the table and moved some chairs in the way.

"Have you seen Mr McDainty?" the headteacher asked, coming towards me. I turned around to face her.

"In his classroom?" I suggested.

"No, only Mr Jenkins is in there," she said. "What a lovely man. I do love the Scottish accent."

I was stunned she hadn't noticed that Mr Jenkins was Mr McDainty in disguise. His accent was terrible! Still, that was one hurdle over. Through the window behind her, I could see Mr McDainty and Miss Bellows slip-sliding their way across the car park to the other side of school.

"He's probably with Mrs Dean," she said, rubbing her chin and looking around.

There was a crash from the kitchen and the sound of metal utensils falling onto the tiled floor rang out. Dave. Mrs Squires made a move towards the kitchen. I had to think quickly.

"It's just some of Year Six helping with the washing up," I said quickly. I hated lying. I guided her away from the door. The pile of skeleton and coat on the floor was moving. Aisha jumped in front of it.

"What's that?" asked Mrs Squires, walking over to the table. My heart started racing and my palms went sweaty. How could we explain a skeleton moving under a coat?

She hadn't spotted that. It was the former Mr Jenkins' arm that she had seen. She picked it up.

"Er, we've been studying skeletons today and that is…er…an example of an arm…"

Mrs Squires examined it.

"It's very realistic." She sniffed it. "Smells of furniture polish," she said, putting it down. "Be careful with it. There's a screw sticking out the end."

"Can we show you our snowpeople we made?" I said.

We needed to get her away from Dave and the fidgeting Mr Jenkins under the table. I also thought it would give Miss Bellows more time to become Mrs Dean. As we headed towards the door, I glanced back and saw Mr Jenkins' left arm reach up and take the right arm off the table. There was another clatter from the kitchen.

Chapter 16
An Unexpected Mrs Dean

In the playground, Danny and Arthur were by a particularly large snowman...I mean, person. We pointed out the different people and Frank was very excited to show her the one he had made.

"We had to start again as the first one we made got destroyed by Mr..."

Oomph!

Danny had thrown a snowball at him to get him to stop talking.

"Hey!" Frank shouted.

"Danny Clarkson! No throwing snowballs!" thundered Mrs Squires.

I looked at the snow figure next

to Danny and Arthur. I spotted the thin
white arms sticking out the sides, with
the bony fingers on the end. So that's
where they hid Mrs Dean. They looked
pleased with themselves. I gave them a
thumbs up.

We continued across the
playground and up the steps to the
classrooms on the far side. As we
reached the Year Four classroom, I
stopped in shock. Miss Bellows greeted

us outside the classroom.

Oh no! She hadn't had time to change!

"Mrs Squires, please let me introduce Mrs Dean to you." Miss Bellows opened the classroom door. We all followed the headteacher into the classroom.

Standing at the interactive whiteboard in front of the Year Six and Four children was a tall, grey-haired lady.

Mrs Squires walked towards her with her hand out. "Lovely to meet you, Mrs Dean. Thank you for helping out today."

Mrs Dean had a strange, high-pitched voice, "Oh, thank you."

I put my head in my hands at the sight of Mr McDainty in a long dress and

grey wig. He was not going to get away
with it this time.

He took the headteacher's hand
and Mrs Squires looked uncertainly at
the large, manly-looking hand that was
thrust into hers.

"Well, I see that everything is
under control here," she said, looking
intently at 'Mrs Dean'.

"I'll just speak to Mr McDainty and then I'll be off. Do you know where he is?"

"No, I haven't seen him since lunch," said 'Mrs Dean' in her high voice.

"Are you from Scotland as well?" Mrs Squires asked.

Miss Bellow's stepped forward. "Why don't we try the hall, Mrs Squires?"

Once they left the room, we rushed to Mr McDainty to help him out of the dress and wig. Thankfully, he was wearing his other clothes underneath.

"Thank you, children!" he said. "That was a close call."

He moved swiftly, out of the door and down the steps into the playground. We watched him stride across the playground and through the doors on the other side.

"Do you think we've got away with it?" asked Aisha.

Chapter 17
Goodbye Mr Jenkins

Once Mrs Squires had left, the former Mr Jenkins came back into the classroom. He was still looking a bit dazed by the rice pudding and hiding incidents and so he sat down while we sang songs. This seemed to perk him up. Especially at heads, shoulders, knees and toes. He joined in with the actions for that one. But only with the one arm.

At about 2.45 pm, Mr McDainty appeared in our classroom.

"It's time for Mr Jenkins to head off now," he said and gestured for the former Mr Jenkins to join him.

"Lazy bones," muttered Danny to Arthur who almost choked trying not to laugh.

"Children, say thank you to Mr Jenkins for looking after you."

We all chorused in the slow, sing-song way that children do when saying things in unison:

"Thank you, Mis-ter Jen-kins"

Aisha put up her hand.

"Yes, Aisha?" asked Mr McDainty

"Where are they going?" she asked.

"Away. Into storage. They'll be perfectly fine until the next time they are required," Mr McDainty said, supposedly reassuringly, but not very informatively.

The former Mr Jenkins gave the class a nod and a wave of the arm he was holding and left the room.

We could hear his clip-clopping feet retreating down the corridor.

I assumed the former Mrs Dean and Dave were going with him. I wondered where they were going. A vision flashed into my mind of that locked door in the corridor of the old part of school.

Could it be?

Skeletons in the closet?

Chapter 18
"Don't Remember"

"Well, that was interesting," Danny said, breaking the silence and my thoughts.

"Yeah, what an unusual day," said Aisha. "Glad I came in now."

"Do you remember that bit where he..." Arthur broke off laughing, "...he fell down those steps into the snowman!"

"And his arm came off!" Danny added. They were laughing hard.

"And...and his...hee hee...foot got stuck in the door...HA!"

"Lots of LOLs!" Danny laughed.

"He took it quite calmly I thought," I said, smiling as I remembered the skeleton picking himself out of the snow.

"Well," Danny said, "nothing gets under his skin."

This sent Arthur and Danny back into hysterics.

It's not that I don't have a sense of humour. I just prefer something a little less cheesy. It's the sort of thing my dad would come out with.

"Still, that was the best day ever," Arthur said, wiping his eyes.

"It was pretty cool," I agreed.

"I wonder if there will be more snow tomorrow?" Aisha asked, looking out the window.

The sun was out and there was water dripping off the roof and the sound of water running into drains.

"I don't think so," I said. "But we'll always have these memories of the snow day and the skeleton staff."

"Yeah, I don't think I'll ever forget the skeleton staff. That was awesome,"

Danny said.

"And Mr McDainty dressed as a woman!" Arthur said.

"That accent was terrible," I said, shaking my head.

The bell rang for the end of the day. Miss Bellows came in and we lined up to be dismissed.

"Well, have a lovely evening, children, and I'll see you all tomorrow for a nice, *normal* school day. No skeleton staff tomorrow." She paused and examined us all.

"Remember, keep what *actually* happened to yourselves," she added. "I don't think your parents, Mrs Willis or Mrs Squires would understand. Do you?" She dismissed us and we all ran out into the playground.

As the snow was melting my mum

arrived without the sledge. Frank was disappointed and let the whole playground know about it. Mum gave us hugs and started with her usual interrogation.

"Did you have fun today?" She asked.

"It was OK," I said.

"Yeah, it was amazing!" Frank shouted.

"What did you do?" she asked hopefully.

"Not much," I said.

Frank was more forthcoming. "We built a snowman."

"Snowperson," I interrupted.

"Snowperson, and we had hot chocolate and played games!" Frank continued loudly.

"Sounds fun," my mum said, beaming. "How were the 'skeleton staff'?"

I laughed, "Oh, Mum, it was just the teachers."

The quizzing continued. "Which teachers were there today?"

Me and Frank looked at each other.

"Don't remember," we said in unison.

My mum sighed and we headed home through the melting slush.

The End

Also available:

The Girl in the Mirror
An Arabian tale for the modern age.

Spending the holidays with Grandma in an antique shop in London isn't very exciting for a 14-year-old girl whose parents have gone to Cairo. All Tamsin wants is an adventure—and maybe to meet a cute boy. Her wish for excitement is granted when she is sent an old Arabian storybook that holds the key to unlocking an ancient treasure.

When 15-year-old Amir comes to the shop, under suspicious circumstances, Tamsin is intrigued by him. After Tamsin's Grandma disappears, Tamsin seeks him out. Aided by an enchanted princess, a child genie, and some unexpected magic, they find themselves hunting for treasure beneath the streets of Cairo and embark on a journey that takes them to the Nile and into the heart of the Pyramids. Now they must uncover the secret of the treasure and stop it from falling into the wrong hands before it's too late.

Available from Amazon as paperback and eBook.

Animal Stories on Stage

20 children's plays based on animal stories

By

Julie Meighan

First published in 2018
by
JemBooks
Cork,
Ireland

dramastartbooks.com

ISBN: 978-0-9935506-5-2

ABOUT THE AUTHOR

Julie Meighan is a lecturer in Drama in Education at the Cork Institute of Technology. She has taught Drama to all age groups and levels. She is the author of the Amazon bestselling *Drama Start: Drama Activities, Plays and Monologues for Young Children (Ages 3 -8)* ISBN 978-0956896605, *Drama Start Two: Drama Activities and Plays for Children (Ages 9-12)* ISBN 978-0-9568966-1-2 and *Stage Start: 20 Plays for Children (Ages 3-12)* ISBN 978-0956896629.

CONTENTS

INTRODUCTION

This book consists of twenty children's plays that are based on classic animal stories. Each play is between five and ten minutes long. The plays can be used for performance, readers' theatre or to promote reading in groups. The plays are simple, so it is very easy for young children to memorise their lines. The cast list is flexible – more characters can be added, and existing characters can be changed or omitted depending on the size and requirements of the group. Most of the characters can be on stage throughout the play, with children walking to the centre of the stage when it is time to say their lines. The teacher/leader can assume the role of the storyteller/s if the children can't read or are not at the reading level required.

Props/costumes/stage directions:

There is a minimal number of props required to stage these plays. The costumes for all the plays are or can be very simple. For example, the children can just wear a colour that represents their animal, wear a mask or use some face paint. A word of advice: if the children wear masks, make sure they don't cover their mouths as it would make it difficult to hear them speak. All suggestions for stage directions are included in brackets and italics.

I hope you enjoy performing or reading the following plays as much as my drama groups have over the years.

BREAK A LEG!

THE DONKEY AND THE WOLF

Characters: Two storytellers, Donkey, Wolf.

Storyteller 1: One day a donkey was happily grazing in a field.

Storyteller 2: Suddenly she heard a snarl.

Donkey: Oh my, what's that noise

Storyteller 1: She looked up and saw a vicious wolf running towards her.

Wolf: I'm very hungry, I'm going to eat that donkey.

Donkey: Oh dear, it's too late to run. I can see his mouth watering. What am I going to do? I must think quickly.

Storyteller 2: Just as the wolf got near her. She said....

Donkey: Ouch, my poor hoof.

Wolf: Whatever is the matter?

Donkey: There is a thorn in my hoof. Can you help get it out? It hurts.

Wolf: (*looks confused*) I'm going to eat you. The thorn in your foot is the least of your worries.

Donkey: Well, if you want to eat me, may I'd suggest you help me. Remove the thorn or else it will get stuck in your throat.

Wolf: Why how very thoughtful of you, Donkey. I do like a considerate lunch. Let me have a look.

Donkey: It is very small, you will have to move closer to see it.

Wolf: I can't see it.

Donkey: It is buried deep in my foot.

Wolf: I still can't see it.

Donkey: Wolf, you will have to move closer.

Storyteller 1: The wolf moved closer and closer.

Storyteller 2: And just as his nose touched the Donkey's foot, she said...

Donkey: Wolf, do you know why you can't see the thorn?

Wolf: No, why can't I see it?

Donkey: Because it isn't there.

Storyteller 1: The Donkey kicked the wolf as hard as she could.

(Wolf flies backwards.)

Wolf: That hurt, Donkey.

Donkey: Hee haw, hee haw. I do like a considerate wolf.

Wolf: I guess I'm not that hungry after all.

(Wolf hangs his head in shame and the donkey continues grazing the field.)

Storyteller: The moral of the story is think before you act.

THE FARMYARD COCKEREL AND THE WEATHERCOCK

Characters: Two Storytellers, Cucumber, Wind, Rain, Hens (as many as you want), Cockerel, Weathercock.

Storyteller 1: Once upon a time there was a cucumber.

Storyteller 2: The Cucumber lived in a vegetable patch near a farmhouse. One day she wondered....

Cucumber: I wonder who is the most useful the farmyard cockerel or the weathercock that sits on top of the farmer house. Mmmmm, I think it is the cockerel, as he wakes everyone up in the morning with his crowing. He also helps to make chickens and they lay eggs. The weathercock is just selfish it just sits on top of the roof and just thinks about himself. I'm very happy with my decision that the cockerel is far more useful than the weathercock.

Storyteller 1: That very night....

Wind: Come on, Rain. I'm bored. Let's do some damage.

Rain: I'm tired just go to sleep. You are always causing mischief.

Wind: Rain, why do always rain on my fun?

Rain: Alright then, just this once.

(They start doing a dance around the cockerel, chicken and hens. The cockerel, chicken and hens are scared, and they huddle together for safety.)

Chicken and Hens: Go away, Wind and Rain you are scaring us.

Weathercock: Wind, Rain you don't scare me. I've been up here for a long time. I'm old stiff and rusty. There is t anything you can do to me.

Storyteller 2: The next morning, the sun was shining, and the sky was clear. The cockerel, chicken and hens all came out from hiding.

Weathercock: I really dislike those pesky birds. They are silly. The world is no good.

Cockerel: Don't be scared chickens. One day you will grow up to be big and strong like me.

Weathercock: Oh, here comes the Cockerel playing the big I am. What's he good for, he can't even lay an egg.

Wind: That weathercock never stops complaining. I'll show him

(The wind howls around the weathercock and the weathercock breaks and tumbles on the ground.

Cockerel: Oh look, chickens, the weathercock has finally broken.

Storyteller 1: The cock, the hens and the chicken she pecked and scratched around the weathercock.

Storyteller 2: The moral of the story is you are no good to anyone if you wear yourself out.

THE BUTTERFLY

Characters: Storyteller, Butterfly, Lady Butterfly, Man, Woman, Daisy, Snowdrop, Violet, Tulip, Sweet Pea. Sweet Pea's mother, Apple Blossom.

Storyteller: There was once a butterfly who desperately wanted to fall in love.

Butterfly: How I long to fall in love and marry the perfect wife.

(Lady Butterfly flies on stage.)

Lady Butterfly: You can marry me if you like. It would be my pleasure to be your wife.

Butterfly: *(looks at her in disgust)* Marry you. Don't make me laugh. I want to marry something very beautiful like a flower.

Lady Butterfly: How dreadfully rude. I've changed my mind. I wouldn't marry you if you were the last butterfly on the planet.

Storyteller: The Lady Butterfly flew off in a huff.

Butterfly: *(rolls his eyes to heaven.)* Good riddance.

(Man walks by with a daisy in his hand. He is pulling off the Daisy's petals one by one.)

Man: She loves me, she loves me not, she loves me, she loves me not, she loves me, she loves me not, she loves me, she loves me not, she loves me, she loves me not, she loves me, she loves me not, she loves me, she loves me not.

Butterfly: Man, what are you doing?

Man: I'm asking the Daisy if the girl I love, loves me back. The Daisy is the wisest flower of them all. Don't you know that?

Storyteller: The butterfly flapped around until he met a wise old Daisy.

Butterfly. Please Daisy, tell me which flower I should marry. There are so many flowers to choose from.

Daisy: My dear, I don't think any flower would want to marry a butterfly.

Butterfly: How rude. I should think any flower should be lucky to have me as a husband.

Butterfly: Snowdrop, will you marry me.

Snowdrop: Its only spring I'm far too young to marry you.

Butterfly: Violet, will you marry me?

Violet: My scent is far too strong for you. You wouldn't be able to live with the smell.

Butterfly: Tulip, will you marry me?

Tulip: My colours are too strong, they would eventually blind you.

Butterfly: Apple Blossom marry me?

Apple blossom: I'm far too delicate. The wind will destroy me. Surely you want your marriage to last.

Butterfly: Sweet Pea marry me?

Sweet Pea: Yes, I'll marry you.

Butterfly: Who is this? *(Points to a drivelled up sweet pea.)*

Sweet Pea's Mother: I'm her mother. She too will one-day look like me.

Butterfly: Oh dear, I've changed my mind. I think it's time to leave.

Storyteller: The butterfly flew off in horror. Spring, passed, summer came and went, and autumn flew by. It was winter, and the butterfly was nowhere nearer to finding a wife.

Butterfly: I don't think I will ever find a wife. *(Sighs and drops his head in despair.)*

Storyteller: One cold winters evening in saw a warm fire through a window. The window was slightly ajar, and he flew in and warmed himself by the fire.

Butterfly: How nice and cosy this room is.

Woman: What a beautiful butterfly. Look at his amazing colours.

Man: *(grabs the butterfly)* Here I've caught him for you. I'll pin home to this cardboard and put him on the wall. You can admire his beauty forever.

Butterfly: Now I'm stuck like all those flowers. This isn't fun.

Storyteller: Soon the butterfly realised something.

Butterfly: Beauty isn't enough to make you happy. To be happy you must have freedom and sunshine.

THE MONKEY AND THE JEALOUS CAMEL

Characters: Three storytellers, Monkey, Giraffe, Lion, Kangaroo, Crocodile, Penguin, Monkey, Camel, Frog, Pig, Squirrel, Ant.

Storyteller 1: Once upon a time a long time ago.

Storyteller 2: All the animals in the world decided to have a big party to celebrate the midsummer.

Storyteller 3: It was a midsummer party and all the animals in the world were going.

Storyteller 1: From the tiniest ant to the enormous elephant.

Storyteller 2: The animals arrived Two by two.

(Everyone sings the animals arrived two by two hurrah hurrah.)

Storyteller 3: Eventually, all the animals had arrived.

(Monkey is ticking off the all the names as the animals enter. He has a click board and looks very official. Giraffe is the look out.)

Monkey: Is that everyone?

Giraffe: I think so, I can't see anyone else coming.

Lion: Well, let's get this party started. Welcome, everyone to this party to celebrate the midsummer. I hope everyone will have wonderful time tonight. I want to introduce the band. Back by popular demand all the way from the Jungle. I would like to introduce our band- the animals.

(Everyone cheers, and claps Elephant is playing her trumpet with his trunk, the bear is playing the drums with his feet. Other animal musical instruments.)

Storyteller 1: Everyone danced and chatted and had a merry time.

(Music playing.)

Kangaroo: Stop the music. I just noticed that the camel isn't here.

Crocodile: Never mind him, he is so grumpy.

Penguin: He couldn't be bothered coming.

Giraffe: No wait, I see something coming up in the hill in the distance.

(Monkey climbs up the tree.)

Monkey: It is the camel and he doesn't look very happy.

(The camel trundles up the hill very slowly)

Penguin: We should be very welcoming to him, when he arrives.

(Camel eventually makes his way up the hill.)

Animals: Hello Camel, welcome to the midsummer's eve party.

Lion: Come and join us.

Camel: *(sighs and wipes his brow.)* This better be a good party. I have come an awfully long way.

Frog: It will be wonderful. Let's play a game of leap frog,

(All the animals jump over one another.)

Pig: That was fun but now let's play piggy in the middle.

(All the animals throw a ball and the pig tries to catch it.)

Storyteller 2: Everyone had so much fun.

Storyteller 3: Then the dolphins performed a lovely water display.

(Music is playing.)

Monkey: now it my turn to show my contemporary dance.

Storyteller 1: The monkey danced, and all the other animals were impressed.

(All the animals cheer and clap when the monkey is finished.)

Pig: That was amazing.

Frog: You are such a good dancer,

Camel: Harrumph! What's all the clapping and cheering about. Anyone can dance like that.

Kangaroo: That's not true. The monkey is a very good dancer.

Ant: You are such a grumpy all hump, Camel.

Elephant: You are just jealous Camel, everyone knows camels can't dance.

Camel: Of course, Camels can dance.

Monkey: Go on then, show us how camels can dance.

(The Camel slowly makes his way to the middle of the circle. All the animals are staring at him and there is a deafening silence.)

Penguin: Band, Music please.

Storyteller 1: The band started to play, and the camel started to dance.

Storyteller 2: It was the most peculiar dance they had ever seen.

(Camel gives a sideways hop and wiggle and then falls over and he bashes into the band and the music stops.)

Squirrel: Watch where you are going.

(The camel does a high kick and hits the kangaroo.)

Kangaroo: Ouch. *(Kangaroo starts limping.)*

Storyteller 3: The camel swings his tail and the rabbit is knocked to the floor.

Storyteller 1: Then, he nearly trod on the ants.

Ant/s: Oh, my goodness. Somebody stop him before he kills us.

(The camel is so clumsy that all the animals scatter to the far side of the stage.)

Lion: *(roars)* Stop! Stop Camel.

Camel: But I'm in the middle of my dance. Can't you see I'm the best dancer here.

Storyteller 1: Then, the unimaginable happened.

Storyteller 2: He stood on the lion's tail.

Lion: *(roars).*

(All the animals freeze.)

Camel: Is it just me? But I get the feeling you didn't like my dance Lion. (Looks around.) why is anyone clapping.

Pig: Your dancing is ......horrible.

Camel:*(hangs his head) I must admit that it wasn't as fun as the monkey's dance. (Looks at the monkey)* You dance very well, Monkey.

Monkey: Thank you. You have special talents too. You can walk for miles without water and you can give everyone rides on your hump.

Kangaroo: Everyone has a talent.

Lion: The world would be a strange place if we all good at the same thing.

Camel: I guess you are right. Well who would like on my hump.

All animals: Me.

Camel: Hop on then.

Storyteller 1: The camel smiled with pride and pleasure.

Storyteller 2: The moral of the story is

Storyteller 3: Everyone is good at something.

THE MONKEY AND THE CROCODILE

Characters: Three storytellers, the crocodile, the crocodile's wife and the monkey.

Storyteller 1: Once upon a time there lived a crocodile that lived in the river Ganges in India.

(Crocodile enters stage swimming slowly.)

Storyteller 2: On both sides of the Ganges there were large music fruit trees.

Storyteller 3: A monkey lived in one of the trees. He ate fruit all day.

(Monkey mimes eating fruit.)

Monkey: These fruits are so delicious and juicy I'm so lucky to live in a fruit tree.

(Crocodile sits under the tree for shade.)

Crocodile: It is very hot I think I will sit under this tree and sleep in the shade. *(Looks up.)* The fruits on tree look so delicious. I wish I could climb the tree and pick some.

Monkey: *(climbs down from the tree)* Since you are resting under my tree, you are my guest. Please come and taste some of my delicious fruits.

Narrator: The monkey plucked the juiciest fruit off the tree and gave it to the crocodile.

Crocodile: Oh, thank you Monkey you are so kind.

Monkey: You are welcome. Come again, any time.

Storyteller: Soon, the crocodile came every day. They would eat the fruit and talk to one another for hours.

(Crocodile and the monkey mime having a conversation and eating lots of fruits.)

Storyteller: One day as the crocodile was leaving to swim home. The monkey gave him some fruit.

Monkey: Crocodile give these fruits to your wife. I plucked them especially for her.

Storyteller: The crocodile swam home and gave the fruit to his wife, she was very happy.

(Crocodile swims home and gives his wife the fruit.)

Crocodile's wife: These fruits are delicious. I have never tasted such sweet fruit in all my life. Where did you get them from?

Crocodile: I got them from my friend the monkey. He lives in the fruit tree, so he knows which ones are the sweetest.

Crocodile's wife: Does the monkey eat fruit every day?

Crocodile: Yes, only the sweetest and juiciest ones. Why do you ask?

Crocodile's wife: Because that means his heart must be so sweet. If I eat his heart I would remain young and beautiful forever. You must steal the monkey's heart and give it to me.

Crocodile: But he is my good friend. He is my only friend. It would be unfair for me to steal his heart.

Crocodile's wife: *(gets angry)* If you loved me you would do it.

Crocodile: Do not get anger my dear, I will do as you wish.

Storyteller: The next day the crocodile swam to the riverbank and reached the tree where the monkey lived.

Monkey: Crocodile, you are late today. I thought you weren't coming.

Crocodile: My wife has made a meal for you. She has invited you to tea because she wants to thank you for giving her your beautiful sweet fruit.

Monkey: That's very kind of her but I'm a land animal, I can't swim.

Crocodile: We live on a sand bank just jump on my back and I'll take you there.

Storyteller: The monkey hopped on the crocodile's back and away they went.

Monkey: Slow down, Croc. You are going too fast.

Crocodile: I'm sorry Monkey but I must go fast because my wife wants to eat your heart for her tea.

Monkey: Oh Croc, you should have told me this before we left. I always keep my heart in the hollow of the tree for safe keeping.

Crocodile: I'll take you back to the tree and you can collect your heart.

Monkey: That would be great.

Storyteller: Crocodile turns and swims back to the tree where the monkey lives upon reaching the bank the monkey jumps off the crocodiles back and clambers up the tree. After a while the crocodile says....

Crocodile: Monkey, you must have found your heart by now. My wife will get angry if we don't arrive soon.

Monkey: You are so foolish crocodile. Don't you know your heart is within yourself? It was a trick to save my life. Now leave my tree and never come back again.

Storyteller: The crocodile left empty handed.

(Crocodile's wife looks very angry.)

Storytellers: The moral of the story is at times presence of mind pays well.

THE RABBIT AND THE LION

Characters: Three narrators, the rabbit, the lion, deer, elephant.

Narrator1: Once upon a time in a jungle in India.

Narrator 2: There lived a lion. He was very powerful and very cruel.

Narrator 3: He hunted and killed a lot of animals in the jungle. Sometimes he just hunted and killed for fun.

Rabbit: We must stop this unnecessary killing.

Elephant: How can we stop the lion? He is too powerful.

Deer: Why don't we have a meeting with the lion?

Fox: And see if we can reach an agreement.

Narrator 1: So, all the animals in the jungle gathered together and invited the lion to the meeting.

Lion: What do you want?

Rabbit: Your majesty we are happy for you to be the King of the Jungle.

Deer: We are happy for you to rule the jungle,

Elephant: We understand that you need to kill us for food.

Lion: Why, that is most kind and understanding of you.

Rabbit: But you are killing animals for fun and not when you are hungry. And if you don't stop there won't be any animals left in jungle.

Lion: Well, what do you suggest?

Rabbit: We decided that we will send you an animal a day to your den. You can kill and eat it. You won't have to go to the bother of hunting.

Lion: Well, that sounds like a clever idea.

Narrator 3: The day arrived where it was the rabbits turn to go to the lion's den.

Rabbit: I don't want to go.

Other animals: You must go if you don't go he will kill the other animals. It was your idea.

Rabbit: I better go then.

Lion: Why are you late?

Rabbit: *(out of breath)* Your majesty it was not my fault. Another lion chased me no wanted to eat me. He said he was king of the jungle.

Lion: I'm the only King of the Jungle. Who is he? Take me to him at once. I shall kill him.

Rabbit: Come with me. I will show you where he lives.

Narrator1: The lion followed the rabbit through the jungle.

Narrator 2: They reached a well.

Rabbit: He lives here.

Narrator 3: The rabbit roared and considered the well. He saw his own reflection looking back at him.

Lion: I see him.

Rabbit: There can only be one King of the jungle. You must kill him.

Narrator 1: The lion jumped into the well and was taken away.

(The rabbit went off and told his friends what had happened.)

(They all had a big party to celebrate.)

THE ELEPHANTS AND THE MICE

Characters: Three storytellers, King Mouse, King Elephant, King, six elephants, six mice, four soldiers.

Storyteller 1: Once upon a time in India there was an earthquake.

Storyteller 2: It left a village in ruins.

Storyteller 3: There was damaged houses and rubble everywhere.

Storyteller 1: All the villagers had left, and the village was deserted except for a group of mice.

(The mice come scurrying on the stage.)

Mouse 1: How lucky we are that we found these ruins to live in.

Mouse 2: We are safe here. Nobody will ever bother us.

Mouse 3: *(suddenly, there was a thumping noise.)* What's that noise?

Mouse 4: Oh no, it is a herd of elephants. Everyone quick hide. *(All the mice hide around the stage.)*

(Elephants come stomping on to the stage.)

Storyteller 2: There was a lake next to the village.

Storyteller 3: The elephants had no choice but to walk through the village.

Elephant 1: I'm thirsty.

Elephant 2: We are nearly at the lake.

Elephants 3: All we need to do is pass these ruins.

Elephants 4: What's that under my feet?

Elephant 5: It is only some mice.

Elephant 6: Just step over them.

(The mice try to avoid the elephants by running around the stage.)

Mouse 5: Wow! That was close *(he wipes his brow.)*

Mouse 6: We can't keep avoiding the elephants. They are going pass here every day to get to the lake.

Mouse 1: I agree, I think we should have a meeting with the king of the mice.

(The king of the mice enters, and all the mice bow.)

King Mouse: You wish to speak to me.

Mouse 2: Yes, your majesty. We have a problem.

King Mouse: How can I help?

Mouse 3: The elephants come through the village and they don't look where they are going.

Mouse 4: If they don't stop they will trample us all.

Mouse 5: King Mouse you must do something

Mouse 6: Or else we will all die

King Mouse: I shall ask the King of the Elephants to help us.

(King Elephants walks on stage.)

King Elephant: I hear you want my help.

King Mouse: *(bows)* Yes, your majesty. We live in the ruins of the village which is near the big lake where the elephants drink their water but every time the herd of elephants pass the village they trample the mice with their massive feet.

King Elephant: What would you like me to do? The elephants must go to the lake to drink the water and bathe.

King Mouse: All you need to do is suggest they change their route.

King Elephant: Why should they?

King Mouse: Because one day the mice could help you.

King Elephant: *(Laughing)* You mice are too small to help giants like us. I will change the route because you made me laugh so much.

King Mouse: Thank you so much, King Elephant.

Storyteller 1: The elephants changed their route and no longer went through the ruined village.

Storyteller 2: There was a king in a nearby kingdom who decided he needed more elephants for his army.

King: Soldiers, you need to capture more elephants.

Soldiers: Yes, your majesty.

(They go off into the jungle and capture the elephants with nets.)

Soldier 1: I think we have captured enough elephants now.

Soldier 2: The king will be very pleased with us.

Soldier 3: I'm hungry. Let's get something to eat and we can come back later and get the elephants.

Soldier 4: They will never escape from this net.

(Soldiers leave the elephants and move to the other side of the stage and mime eating.)

Elephant 1: What are we going to do?

Elephant 2: We will never get out of here.

King Elephant: I have an idea.

(He trumpets loudly, and the mice come in.)

King Mouse: King Elephant, you called.

King Elephant: The king's soldiers captured us. We are stuck in this net and we can't get out.

King Mouse: Come on, mice. Let's bite through the ropes and free the elephants.

Storyteller 1: Eventually, the elephants broke free.

Storyteller 2: They were very happy, and they thanked the mice for their help.

Storyteller 3: The lesson of this story is never estimate people.

ANDROCLES AND THE LION

Characters: Two storytellers, Androcles, Lion, Emperor, three slaves, three roman guards and as many spectators as you wish.

Storyteller 1: A long, long time ago when the Romans ruled the world.

Storyteller 2: There lived a slave called Androcles.

(Androcles walks on the stage and addresses the audience.)

Androcles: Hello everyone, I'm Androcles. I'm a slave. Life is not so good when you are a slave. I work hard and I'm always hungry. *(He mimes digging and he wipes his brow.)*

(Enter slaves and guards. The slaves mime doing manual jobs while the guards observe.)

Guard 1: Slaves, work harder. Any slacking and you will be fed to the hungry lions in the arena.

Androcles: I can't take this life anymore.

Slave 1: Androcles, we are slaves.

Slave 2: We must do as the Romans tell us.

Slave 3: You should learn to accept your fate.

Androcles: I don't want to accept this terrible life. I'm going to escape. I need you to cause a distraction.

Slave 1: I'll do it. *(He collapses in pain and the guards run towards him.)*

Guard 2: Stop that noise at once.

Guard 3: What is the matter with you?

Slave 1: I've twisted my ankle.

Slave 2: Go now and good luck.

Slave 3: Don't get caught or else you will be fed to the lions in the arena.

(They hug quickly and Androcles escapes without the guards noticing.)

Storyteller 1: Androcles jumped over the wall.

Storyteller 2: And ran through the forest.

Androcles: I'm exhausted. *(He stretches, yawns and looks around.)* This looks like a good place to sleep.

Storyteller 1: Androcles was just about to lie down when he heard a loud roar.

Lion: Roarrrrrrrrrrrrrrrrrrrrrrr!

Androcles: It's a lion. Oh dear, he looks very angry.

Lion: I'm not angry. I've got this thorn stuck in my paw. I'm in pain. Roarrrrrrrrrrrrrrrrrrrrrrr!

Androcles: I'll help you.

Storyteller 2: Androcles pulled the thorn out of the Lion's paw.

Androcles: There you go. I'll put some leaves on it to keep it dry.

Lion: Thank you so much I was in so much pain. Maybe one day I'll return your good deed.

Storyteller 1: Years passed but one-day Androcles' luck ran out. *(Androcles is casually walking around the stage.)*

Guard 1: Caught you at last.

Guard 2: Your luck has finally run out.

Guard 3: The emperor is very angry with you.

(Enter Emperor.)

Emperor: Slave, you are going to pay for escaping. Guards, take him to the arena and throw him to the lions. I could do with something to amuse me.

(Guards throw Androcles into the arena.)

Guard 1: Enjoy.

Guard 2: See you later.

Guard 3: Ha, ha I doubt we will ever see him again, alive.

Storyteller 2: Androcles waited in the arena for the trapdoor to open. The crowd cheered loudly.

Androcles: This is the end for me. I'll just close my eyes. I hope it will be quick.

(The trapdoor open and the lion comes out roaring but then he sees Androcles with his eyes closed.)

Spectators: Kill him, kill him, kill him.

(The lion walks slowly towards Androcles whose eyes are still firmly shut.)

Lion: Open your eyes, Androcles.

Androcles: No, just eat me and get it over with.

Spectators: Kill him, kill him, kill him.

Lion: Androcles, it is I the lion you helped in the forest. I would never eat you.

Storyteller 1: Androcles slowly opens his eyes.

Androcles: Hello, my friend. *(They hug.)*

(The spectators cheer)

Emperor: Androcles, you have made friends with a fierce creature. Your reward is your freedom.

Androcles: Emperor, thank you. *(Androcles bows.)*

Storyteller 2: The Lion and Androcles lived to a ripe old age and remained friends.

(They hug and wave at the crowd.)

THE DOG AND HIS REFLECTION

Characters: Narrator, Dog, Cat, Mouse, Cow, Horse, Neighbour, Neighbour's Dog, Dog's Reflection.

Narrator: Once upon a time there was a very greedy dog that would eat anything.

Dog: I'm so hungry all the time. All I do during day is think about food and all I do at night is dream about food.

(Cat walks onto the stage stealthily.)

Cat: I'm looking forward to my lovely saucer of milk.

(Dog sneaks up behind Cat and drinks his bowl of milk very quickly.)

Cat: Where has all my milk gone?

(Dog shrugs his shoulders.)

Dog: I don't know.

Cat: Don't lie to me Dog, you have milk all over your mouth.

(Dog wipes his mouth with his arm and bounds off the stage.)

Cat: This is the third time this week he drank my milk and it's only Tuesday.

(Cat leaves the stage looking sad and disappointed. Mouse creeps in.)

Mouse: I'm looking forward to a nice piece of cheese.

(Dog sneaks up behind Mouse and eats his cheese very quickly.)

(Mouse turns around.)

Mouse: Where is my cheese?

Dog: *(Dog shrugs his shoulders)* I don't know.

Mouse: Don't lie to me Dog. You have cheese all over your mouth.

(Dog wipes his mouth with his arm and bounds off stage.)

Mouse: This is the third time this week he has eaten my cheese and it's only Tuesday.

(Mouse leaves the stage looking sad and disappointed. Cow walks in.)

Cow: I'm looking forward to my freshly cut straw

(Dog sneaks up behind Cow and eats his straw very quickly.)

Cow: Where has my straw gone?

(Dog shrugs his shoulders.)

Dog: I don't know.

Cow: Don't lie to me Dog. You have straw all over your mouth.

(Dog wipes his mouth with his arm and bounds off stage.)

Cow: This is the third time this week he has eaten my straw and it's only Tuesday.

(Cow leaves the stage looking sad and disappointed. Horse gallops in.)

Horse: I'm looking forward to my hay.

(Dog sneaks up behind Horse and eats his hay very quickly.)

Horse: Where has all my hay gone?

(Dog shrugs his shoulders.)

Dog: I don't know.

Horse: Don't lie to me Dog, you have hay all over your mouth.

(Dog wipes his mouth with his arm and bounds off stage.)

Horse: This is the third time this week he has eaten my hay and it's only Tuesday.

(Cat, Cow and Mouse walk on the stage.)

Cat: What are we going to do about Dog? He keeps eating our food.

Mouse: I'm always hungry because I haven't eaten cheese for days.

Horse: I'm wasting away to nothing.

Narrator: Cow who was the wisest animal in the farmyard mooed and said.

Cow: Moo, moo we need to be patient Dog will get his comeuppance in the end.

Cat: Meanwhile we will all die of hunger.

Narrator: One day, Dog went for a walk. He spotted a bone in the neighbour's garden.

The bone was for the neighbour's dog.

Neighbour: I have this lovely juicy bone for your tea. (*Neighbour points to the bone and his dog looks very excited.*)

Neighbour's Dog: Oh, thank you master. I can't wait.

Neighbour: When I've finished cutting the wood we can have it for our tea.

Dog: I'll chase some rabbits to build up my appetite.

(*The neighbour chops wood and his dog chases rabbits.*)

Dog: Now is my chance. I'll take that bone and have it later.

(*He sneaks inside the garden, takes the bone and makes his escape.*)

Dog: This is great. Extra food for me tonight.

Narrator: After a while, Dog came to a small river.

Dog: I must cross this river, so I can get back to the farm and chew on this juicy bone.

Narrator: As he crossed the river, he looked down and saw something very strange.

Dog: Another dog is looking at me with a big bone in his mouth.

(*Dog's Reflection come on the stage with a bone in his mouth and stands opposite Dog.*)

His bone is even bigger and juicier than mine.

I know I'll just take it off him.

Narrator: Dog opened his jaw to grab the other dog's bone. Dog's own bone fell from his mouth and floated down the river. (*The dog's reflection mirrors the dog and drops his bone.*)

Dog: Never mind, it doesn't matter. I'll have a bigger and juicier bone now.

Dog & Dog's Reflection: Where is the bone gone? The dog is still there but he doesn't have his bone. Oh dear, that's not another dog, it's my reflection.

Dog: I feel so foolish I'm not even hungry anymore.

Narrator: That night Cat, Mouse, Cow and Horse ate their food.

Cow: Dog I hope you learned your lesson. It doesn't pay to be greedy. You might lose the good things you already have.

Dog: I'll never be greedy again.

THE JOLLY FARMER AND THE EAGLE

Characters: Jolly Farmer, Eagle, Storyteller, Two Neighbours

Storyteller: Once upon a time there was a farmer. He was always very jolly.

Jolly Farmer: I'm a jolly farmer, and I'm also very hardworking. (*He mimes ploughing the fields, cut down the trees for fire wood, milked cows.*) What a beautiful day. (*He starts singing while he is working.*) I'm finished; it's time to go home.

(*He grabs his things and starts to make his way home.*)

Eagle: Help me, help me.

Farmer: What's that sound? It sounds like a bird in pain. It is coming from over there.

Eagle: Help me, help me. I'm stuck in this trap.

Farmer: Poor eagle. I'll get you out.

Eagle: Please hurry; I'm in pain.

(*The farmer cuts the net with is knife.*)

Farmer: Now you are free. Fly away and be happy.

Eagle: (*Starts crying.*)

Farmer: Don't cry. What's the matter?

Eagle: I'm free but I'm injured. I can't move; my wings hurt.

Farmer: Don't worry, I'll take care of you until you can fly again.

Storyteller: The farmer brought the eagle home and took great care of her.

Farmer: You are getting better every day.

Eagle: You are so kind. I will never forget what you have done for me.

(Knock, knock, there is a knock on the farmer's door.)

Farmer: Hello, neighbours. What can I do for you?

Neighbour 1: We hear you have an eagle?

Neighbour 2: What are you going to do with it?

Neighbour 1: You should sell it. You will get a decent price for it.

Neighbour 2: You should eat it. Eagle meat is delicious.

Farmer: I'm going to let him go.

(Neighbours leave the house, disappointed and confused.)

Neighbours: Why is he letting the eagle go free?

Storyteller: A few days later, the eagle's wing was better.

Eagle: I can fly again.

Farmer: Fly away eagle.

(The eagle flies away.)

Farmer: Look at it fly. What a beautiful bird.

Storyteller: A few days later, the farmer was working in his field. The day grew hotter and hotter and the farmer said...

Farmer: I think I'll take quick nap in the shade by this wall.

Storyteller: He didn't notice that the wall was very shaky and could tumble over at any time.

(The eagle flew over the field where the farmer was working.)

Eagle: Wake up, farmer, quickly.

Farmer: Oh, hello eagle. How are you? What's wrong?

(Eagle snatches the farmer's hat.)

Farmer: Come back.

Eagle: At last, he is following me. I'll drop the hat here.

Farmer: Stop thief.

Farmer: Why did you do that?

(Suddenly there was a crash the old wall tumbled down.)

Farmer: Thanks, eagle. You saved my life.

Eagle: You are welcome. You saved my life; I just returned the favour.

(Eagle flies away.)

Farmer: You are the king of all birds.

THE HUNGRY HYENA

Characters: Two Storytellers, Hyena, Jackal, Three Men, Goats and Sheep (as many as you want)

Storyteller1: Once upon a time on the African plains, there lived a hyena.

Storyteller 2: He was very hungry.

Hyena: I'm so hungry. I haven't eaten for a week. (*He drags himself along the stage looking weak. He rubs his tummy.*)

Storyteller 1: Soon, a jackal passed by and heard a strange noise.

Jackal: What was that noise?

Hyena: It is just my tummy rumbling. I'm so hungry.

Jackal: Well, I know a place where there is lots of food to feast on.

Hyena: I would be grateful if you would show me.

Jackal: Men live there, so we must go there at night and we must be very quiet.

Storyteller 2: That night...

Jackal: We are here.

Hyena: At last.

(*They are hiding behind a bush. Goats and sheep are walking around the stage. The goats are bleating.*)

Hyena: What are these creatures? I've never seen them on the African plains.

Jackal: These are sheep, and these are goats. (*Jackal points to the sheep and then to the goats.*)

Hyena: What are we waiting for? Let's go.

Jackal: A word of warning, Hyena. You must only eat the sheep. The goats bleat very loudly, and they will wake the men up.

Hyena: Thanks for the warning. I'll make sure I just eat the sheep.

Jackal: There is a hole in the fence; we can sneak in there.

(*The goats and sheep yawn and fall asleep; the jackal and hyena tip-toe into the enclosure.*)

Storyteller 1: The hyena couldn't believe his luck. He grabbed a sheep and swallowed him.

Storyteller 2: Then, he swallowed another, and another. (*The sheep don't make a sound.*)

Storyteller 1: Soon, sunrise came.

Jackal: Hyena, we must go back through the hole in the fence.

Hyena: I can barely walk. My tummy is touching the ground. (*The hyena struggles to walk.*)

Jackal: Get a move on. I'm just going to take a quick bite of this goat before I go.

Goat: Bleat, bleat. (*Three men run on to the stage with spears.*)

Man 1: What's that noise?

Man 2: Some wild animals are attacking our livestock.

Man 3: Let's catch them and teach them a lesson.

Jackal: Quick, we need to get out of here, NOW!

Hyena: I'm stuck in the hole. I've eaten too much I can't fit through it. Why did you bite the goat? You knew he would wake the men up.

Jackal: Ha, ha because now the men will think you are the culprit and I can make my escape, ha, ha. They will never catch me.

Man 1: Here he is. (*He grabs the hyena.*)

Man 2: There is the thief.

Man 3: Well, we are going to keep him and make him work here forever to pay back his debt.

Storyteller 2: That night when the Hyena was curled up in cage all alone, he thought to himself.

Hyena: In the future, I should be more careful who I choose as friends.

HOW THE BEAR GOT HIS TAIL

Characters: Storyteller, Little Bear, Mama Bear, Fox, Fisherman, Bear

Storyteller: Once upon a time, there lived a little bear. He was very curious and always asking questions.

Little Bear: Mama Bear, why is the grass green?

Mama Bear: I don't know, Little Bear.

Little Bear: Mama Bear, why is the sky blue?

Mama Bear: I don't know, Little Bear.

Little Bear: Mama Bear, why do bears have short, stumpy tails?

Mama Bear: I know the answer to this question.

Little Bear: You do? (*Looks very shocked.*) Please tell me.

Mama Bear: Bears didn't always have short stumpy tails, you know.

Little Bear: They didn't.

Mama Bear: Once upon a time, all bears had long, fluffy tails.

Little Bear: Whatever happened to them?

Mama Bear: Well, it was all the fox's fault.

(*Fox walks by and interrupts. He is very indignant.*)

Fox: Why is everything always my fault?

Mama Bear: Because it always is. Now, Little Bear, come over here and sit down here and I'll tell you the whole story.

(Fox walks off in a huff.)

Mama Bear: One day, years and years and years ago, when the world was very cold and there was lots of snow and ice. There was a fox.

(Fox walks back on the stage.)

Fox: I'm very hungry, I can't find anything to eat in all this snow and ice.

Mama Bear: Suddenly, she spotted a fisherman fishing in the lake.

Fox: Hello, Fisherman. Have you caught much fish today?

Fisherman: Hello, Fox. I cut a hole in the frozen lake and I've caught lots of fish. Look over here.

(The fox sees lots of fish on the ground.)

Fox: I've a plan. If I'm quick, I can grab the fish and run away.

Mama Bear: And that's exactly what he did.

(Fox runs off with the fish.)

Fisherman: Hey Fox, come back. You have robbed my dinner.

Fox: Ha, ha, the fisherman is so foolish, He should never have trusted a sly old fox like me.

Mama Bear: Soon, along came a bear waving his fluffy tail. He saw the fox holding the fish.

Bear: Fox, where did you get those delicious juicy fish?

Fox: I caught them in the frozen lake.

Bear: I'm hungry. I would love some fish.

Fox: It is very easy to catch them. Cut a hole in the ice and put your tail in the water. The fish will nibble at your tail and then you can catch them.

Bear: That doesn't sound very pleasant. The water is cold and surely all that nibbling will hurt.

Fox: Well, it is cold, and it does hurt a little, but your fluffy tail will catch lots of fish.

Bear: Thank you, Fox.

Mama Bear: So, the bear trundled through the snow to the frozen lake.

Bear: I'll cut the hole in the ice. Then, Fox said to sit on the hole and put my tail in. (*He sits on the hole and puts his tail in.*) I'm so cold. I'll take deep breaths and count to ten: 1, 2, 3, 4.... I can't do it. It hurts too much.

Mama Bear: He tried to pull his tail out of the water, but it was stuck.

Bear: Oh dear, my tail is frozen.

Mama Bear: He pulled and pulled and then he heard an almighty SNAP!

Bear: What was that noise? Oh, my goodness, my tail has snapped off. (*The bear starts to cry.*)

Mama Bear: From that day on, all bears have short, stumpy tails.

(Fox approaches Little Bear and Mama Bear.)

Fox: Little Bear, there is a valuable lesson that all bears should learn from this story.

Little Bear: What should all bears learn from this lesson?

Fox: Never, ever believe everything you are told.

THE BEAR AND THE TRAVELLERS

Characters: Storyteller, Two Travellers, Bear (extra animals such as deer, rabbits, birds, mice can be included)

Storyteller: Once upon a time, there were two friends who liked to travel to weird and wonderful places together.

Traveller 1: My friend, would you like to travel with me to the magical village on the other side of this land?

Traveller 2: I would like nothing more than to have an adventure with you, my friend.

Storyteller: They went off on their adventure together.

Traveller 1: What a wonderful adventure.

Traveller 2: We get to see lots of interesting things on the way.

Traveller 1: Like the beautiful birds in the sky.

Traveller 2: And the friendly deer, rabbits and mice playing happily in the field.

Storyteller: Soon, they came to a wood. There was a big sign at the entrance.

Traveller 1: Danger.

Traveller 2: Beware of bears.

Traveller 1: What should we do?

Traveller 2: We should continue as we have come this far.

Traveller 1: We should walk slowly.

Traveller 2: Try not to make any noise. We should stay close to one another.

Traveller 1: It's getting darker and darker.

Traveller 2: The path is getting smaller and smaller.

Storyteller: What the two travellers didn't know was there was a large brown bear hiding behind a large tree.

Bear: I smell a man or two. There they are. I'll hide behind this tree and jump out and scare them.

Storyteller: So, the bear did just that.

Bear: *(Jumps out from behind the tree.)* Roarrrrrrrrrr.

Traveller 1: Quick, climb a tree quickly!

Traveller 2: I can't climb the tree. Can you help me?

Storyteller: He looked around, but his friend was nowhere to be seen.

Bear: Roar!

Traveller 2: The bear is getting closer. I know - I'll lie on the floor and pretend to be dead.

Bear: I know you aren't dead. I've something very important to tell you. Listen very carefully. I shall say this only once: Never trust someone who leaves you in your hour of need.

(Bear stomps off.)

(Traveller 1 re-emerges.)

Traveller 1: Are you alright, my friend?

Traveller 2: Yes.

Traveller 1: What did the bear whisper to you?

Traveller 2: Just some sound advice, but I'll think I'll keep it to myself.

THE BEGINNINGS OF THE ARMADILLO

Characters: Narrator; Stickly, Prickly Hedgehog; Slow and Solid Tortoise; Painted Jaguar; Monkey; Deer; Beetle; Frog; Mother Jaguar.

Narrator: Once upon a time on the banks of the Turbid Amazon, there lived a Stickly, Prickly Hedgehog.

Hedgehog: Hello, I'm the Stickly, Prickly Hedgehog. I eat shelly snails and things. *(Mimes picking up a snail and bites into it.)* Yummy! *(He rubs his tummy.)* This is my friend, the Slow and Solid Tortoise.

Tortoise: Hello, I'm the Slow and Solid Tortoise. I like to eat green leafy lettuce and things. *(He mimes picking up a head of lettuce and starts to eat it. The hedgehog and the tortoise move to stage left and are playing with each other. The Painted Jaguar enters the stage and moves to the centre.)*

Painted Jaguar: Hello, I'm the Painted Jaguar. I like to eat everything I can catch.

Monkey: Oooh, ooh, ooh, eee, eee, come and catch me, Painted Jaguar.

(Jaguar tries to catch the monkey but fails. The monkey swings from tree to tree.)

Deer: Bleat, bleat, come and catch me, Painted Jaguar.

(Jaguar tries to catch the deer but fails. The deer scampers off.)

Painted Jaguar: *(sighs)* The problem is, I'm not very good at catching anything.

Narrator: He tried to eat a frog.

Frog: Ribbit, ribbit, come and catch me, Painted Jaguar.

(Jaguar tries to catch the frog but fails. The frog hops away.)

Narrator: He tried to catch a beetle.

Beetle: Whoop, whoop, come and catch me, Painted Jaguar.

(Jaguar tries to catch the beetle but fails. The beetle scuttles off.)

Narrator: He couldn't catch any animal and he went home sad and hungry.

Mother Jaguar: You look so sad, dear. What's the matter?

Painted Jaguar: Oh, Mother, I'm so hungry. I tried to catch a monkey, a deer, a frog and a beetle and I failed ... miserably.

Mother Jaguar: Listen carefully. I'll teach you how to catch a hedgehog.

Painted Jaguar: A hedgehog? But he is very prickly and stickly.

Mother Jaguar: That is true but the trick is, when you catch a hedgehog you must drop him into the water. Wait until he panics because he can't swim and then you can eat him.

Painted Jaguar: When you a catch a tortoise, you must scoop him out of his shell with your paw. Just like this. *(She mimes scooping out something with her paws.)*

Narrator: The next night, the Painted Jaguar went looking for the Sticky, Prickly Hedgehog and the Slow and Solid Tortoise. Soon he came across them.

Painted Jaguar: At last I've found you. Just in time. I'm very hungry.

Hedgehog: Oh, dear, we can't run away. He is too fast.

Tortoise: Quickly, curl up. I'll stick my head and feet into my shell.

Painted Jaguar: You two must listen to me. I have something important to say.

Hedgehog: Ignore him.

Tortoise: No problem. *(He starts to put his head in his shell.)*

Painted Jaguar: You can ignore me all you want but my mother told me that when I meet a hedgehog, I'm to drop him into water and he will uncoil. When I meet a tortoise I'm to scoop him into my paw. Now, who is who?

Hedgehog: Are you sure that's what your mother told you?

Painted Jaguar: Quite sure.

Tortoise: Quite sure? I'm sure she might have said that you uncoil the tortoise and shell him out of the water with a scoop.

Hedgehog: And when you paw a hedgehog, you must drop him into your paw.

Tortoise: Maybe she said that when you water a hedgehog you must shell him until he

Painted Jaguar: Oh dear, I'm confused now. I don't know what my mother said.

Hedgehog: Let's explain it more clearly. When you scoop water, you uncoil it.

Tortoise: When you pour meat, you drop it into a tortoise with a scoop.

Hedgehog: Is it clear now?

Painted Jaguar: No, my brain hurts. Just tell me which one of you is the hedgehog and which is the tortoise.

Hedgehog: I couldn't possibly tell you that, but you can scoop me out if you wish.

Painted Jaguar: Then you must be the tortoise.

Narrator: The Painted Jaguar stuck out his paw to scoop out the hedgehog, but just then the hedgehog curled up. The Painted Jaguar's paw was filled with pricks.

Painted Jaguar: Ouch, you are not the tortoise. You are Stickly, Prickly Hedgehog.

Tortoise: I'm the tortoise. If you want to uncoil me, drop me into the water.

Painted Jaguar: You've mixed everything up. I'm so confused. I don't know if I'm on my painted head or painted tail. My mother told me to drop one of you into the water.

(He throws the tortoise into the water. The Painted Jaguar as the Slow and Solid Tortoise swims away.)

Tortoise: You can't catch me now, tortoise.

Hedgehog: Ha, ha, bye-bye, Painted Jaguar.

(The Painted Jaguar returns home weary and dejected.)

Mother Jaguar: What's the matter, son? What have you done to your poor painted paw?

Painted Jaguar: I tried to scoop something that said he wanted to be scooped out of his shell.

Mother Jaguar: Your paw is full of prickles. You must have tried to scoop the hedgehog. You should have dropped the hedgehog into the water.

Painted Jaguar: I did that to the other animal. I haven't eaten all day and I'm sooooo hungry.

Mother Jaguar: Listen carefully. A hedgehog curls in so his prickles stick out and he can't swim.

(Hedgehog and tortoise are hiding in the bushes, listening carefully.) A tortoise cannot curl up, but he can draw his head and legs into his shell. He is a good swimmer.

Painted Jaguar: That's easy. I've got it.

Can't curl but can swim, Slow and Solid Tortoise, that's him.

Curls up but can't swim, Stickly, Prickly Hedgehog, that's him.

Tortoise: He'll never forget that.

Hedgehog: We need to do something.

Tortoise: I'll teach you how to swim

Hedgehog: And I'll teach you how to curl up. That will fool the Painted Jaguar.

Narrator: They practiced by the banks of the Turbid Amazon. *(The tortoise practises curling and the hedgehog practises swimming.)*

Tortoise: We've done it. I can curl, and you can swim.

Hedgehog: You look different.

Tortoise: So, do you.

Narrator: They saw the Painted Jaguar walking along the banks of the river. He was still nursing his sore paw.

Hedgehog: Morning, Painted Jaguar.

Painted Jaguar: Good morning. I know who you are. You are the hedgehog. You can't swim.

Hedgehog: Oh yes, I can. Look.

(Hedgehog jumps in the river and starts swimming.)

Painted Jaguar: You are the tortoise. You can't curl.

Tortoise: Oh yes, I can. Look.

(Tortoise curls up. The Painted Jaguar looks confused and runs off.)

Tortoise & Hedgehog: That got rid of him, ha, ha.

Painted Jaguar: Mother, Mother, there were two animals by the Turbid Amazon. The one you said can't curl, can and the other one who can't swim, can. I'm so confused.

Mother Jaguar: A hedgehog is a hedgehog. A tortoise is a tortoise. They can never be anything else.

Painted Jaguar: They are a bit of both and I don't know their proper names.

Mother Jaguar: Everything should have a name. Let's call them armadillos and you shouldn't touch them.

Narrator: Painted Jaguar did as he was told. Ever since that day, every hedgehog and every tortoise on the Turbid Amazon has been called an armadillo.

Part Two:

Movement Plays

Movement plays are a fun and engaging way to develop children's motor skills. They also help build cooperative learning in the classroom. The teacher/narrator tells a story, a child or a group of children must make a specific action or sound when they hear a certain word in the story. The children must listen very carefully to the story in order to participate fully. These plays can be performed in front of an audience or used as part of a movement or drama class.

GOLDILOCKS AND THE THREE BEARS

Each child finds a space and sits down. Each child or a group of children are assigned a specific word and a corresponding action. The narrator/teacher reads the story aloud, and when the children hear their word, they must jump up and do their actions. The words are in bold to assist the teacher/narrator.

Movement: Action

Goldilocks: Skip around the space.

Bear/Bears: Walk slowly and growl.

Bowl/Bowls: Clasp fingers together and stick out arms to make a round shape.

Porridge: Wiggle body up and down.

Chair/s: Squat down and stick out arms.

Bed/s: Lies straight on the floor.

First: Holds up one finger.

Second: Holds up two fingers.

Third: Holds up three fingers.

Narrator: Once upon a time, there was a girl called **Goldilocks**. One day, she decided to go for a walk in the woods. Soon, she became tired. She saw a little cottage in the woods. She knocked, but there was no answer, so she decided to go inside and rest.

At the table in the kitchen, there were three **bowls** of porridge. **Goldilocks** was hungry. She tasted the **porridge** from the **first bowl**.

"This **porridge** is too hot!" she exclaimed.

So, she tasted the **porridge** from the **second bowl**.

"This **porridge** is too cold," she said.

So, she tasted the **third bowl** of **porridge**.

"Ahhh, this **porridge** is just right," she said happily, and she ate it all up.

After she'd eaten the three bears' breakfasts, she decided she was feeling a little tired. So, she walked into the living room where she saw three chairs. **Goldilocks** sat in the **first chair** to rest her feet.

"This **chair** is too big!" she exclaimed.

So she sat in the **second chair**.

"This **chair** is too big, too!" she whined.

So she tried the **third** and smallest **chair**.

"Ahhh, this **chair** is just right," she sighed. But just as she settled down into the **chair** to rest, it broke into pieces!

Goldilocks was very tired by this time, so she went upstairs to the bedroom. She lay down in the **first bed**, but it was too hard. Then she lay in the **second bed**, but it was too soft. Then she lay down in the **third bed**, and it was just right. **Goldilocks** fell asleep.

As she was sleeping, the three bears came home.

"Someone's been eating my **porridge**," growled the Papa **bear**.

"Someone's been eating my **porridge**," said the Mama **bear**.

"Someone's been eating my **porridge**, and they ate it all up!" cried the Baby **bear**.

"Someone's been sitting in my **chair**," growled the Papa **bear**.

"Someone's been sitting in my **chair**," said the Mama **bear**.

"Someone's been sitting in my **chair**, and they've broken it all to pieces," cried the Baby **bear**.

They decided to look around some more, and when they got upstairs to the bedroom, Papa **bear** growled, "Someone's been sleeping in my **bed**,"

"Someone's been sleeping in my **bed**, too," said the Mama **bear**

"Someone's been sleeping in my **bed**, and she's still there!" exclaimed Baby **bear**.

Just then, Goldilocks woke up and saw the three **bears**. She screamed, "Help!" And she jumped up and ran out of the room. **Goldilocks** ran down the stairs, opened the door, and ran away into the woods. And **Goldilocks** never returned to the home of the three **bears**.

THE LION AND THE MOUSE

Each child finds a space and sits down. Each child or a group of children are assigned a specific word and a corresponding action. The narrator/teacher reads the story aloud, and when the children hear their word, they must jump up and do their actions. The words are in bold to assist the teacher/narrator.

Movement: Action.

Lion: Get down on hands and knees, and move around stealthily as a lion stalking his prey.

Mouse: Scamper like a mouse and squeak.

Forest: Make yourself into a large tree.

Roar/roared/roaring: Roar loudly like a lion.

Eat: Do a gobbling action.

Help: Extend hands in a kindly gesture.

Narrator: One day, a **lion** was fast asleep in the forest, his head resting on his paw and he was snoring away. A timid little **mouse** came scampering by him and accidentally scampered across the **lion's** nose. The lion woke up with a loud **roar**. The **lion** laid his huge paw angrily on the timid little **mouse**. He **roared**, "I'm going to eat you up."

"Don't **eat** me!" begged the poor **mouse**. "Please let me go and someday I will **help** you."

The **lion** was much amused to think that a **mouse** could ever **help** him. But he was generous and finally let the **mouse** go.

Some days later, while walking in the **forest**, the **lion** was caught in a hunter's net. Unable to free himself, he filled the **forest** with his angry **roaring**. The **mouse** heard the roar and quickly found the **lion** trapped in the net. Running to one of the great ropes that bound him, she chewed it until it fell apart, and soon the **lion** was free.

"You laughed when I said one day I would **help** you," said the **mouse**. "Now, you see that even a **mouse** can help a **lion**."

They hugged, and from then on, the **lion** and the **mouse** were very good friends.

THE TORTOISE AND THE HARE

Each child finds a space and sits down. Each child or a group of children are assigned a specific word and a corresponding action. The narrator/teacher reads the story aloud and when the children hear their word they must jump up and do their actions. The words are in bold to assist the teacher/narrator.

Movement: Action.

Boast/boastful/boasting: Stand up straight and puff out chest.

Woods: Children make themselves into trees.

Animals: Each child chooses a different animal found in the woods and moves like that animal.

Hare: Make bunny ears with your hands.

Fast: Children move as fast as they can.

Run: Run on the spot.

Tortoise: Children bend over as if they have something heavy on their back.

Slow: Children move in slow motion around the room.

Narrator: Once upon a time there was a very **boastful hare** that lived in the **woods** with lots of other **animals**. He was always **boasting** about how **fast** he could **run**. He **boasted**, "I'm the **fastest** animal in the woods. No one can **run** as **fast** as me." The other **animals** were tired of listening to him. One day the **tortoise** said to the **hare,** "**Hare** you are so **boastful**. I challenge you to a race." **Hare** laughed and said, "**Tortoise**, you will never beat me. You are too **slow** and steady." They decided whoever got to the other side of the **woods** the **fastest** was the winner. All the other **animals** in the **woods** came to watch the race. The **hare ran** as **fast** as he could through the **woods**. After a while he thought to himself, "I'm so **fast** that **slow** tortoise will never beat me. I think I will take a quick nap." Soon he fell asleep. The **tortoise** walked **slowly** through the **woods**. He passed the sleeping **hare**. The **animals** watched the **tortoise** near the finishing line. The **animals** cheered loudly. The **hare** woke up and **ran** as **fast** as he could through the **woods** to the finishing line, but it was too late. The **slow tortoise** had won the race. All the **animals** in the **woods** congratulated the **tortoise**. The **hare** had to remind himself that he shouldn't **boast** about his **fast** pace because **slow** and steady won the race.

THE THREE LITTLE PIGS

Each child finds a space and sits down. Each child or a group of children are assigned a specific word and a corresponding action. The narrator/teacher reads the story aloud and when the children hear their word they must jump up and do their actions. The words are in bold to assist the teacher/narrator.

Movement: Action.
Any number: Show that number of fingers.
Little: Crouch down as small as you can.
Pig: Get on all fours and oink once.
Pigs: Get on all fours and oink twice.
Big: Stretch up as high as you can.
Bad: Make an angry face.
Wolf: Make hands into claws and say "aargh."
Laughing: Laugh loudly.
Smiling: Big wide smile.
Trotted: Trot up and down the space.
Straw: Rub your hands together.
Sticks: Clap your hands together.
Bricks: Clap your hands on your thighs.
Huff/huffed: Blow.
Puff/puffed: Blow harder.

Blow\blew: Stamp feet on the ground.

Narrator: Once upon a time there was a mother **pig** that lived with her **three little pigs**. One day she said "**Little pigs,** I think it is time for you to leave and make your own way in this **big** world. You each need to build your own **house.**" The little pigs were very excited about their new, **big** adventure. Mother **pig** gave each of her **little pigs** a hug, but she warned them "Remember to watch out for the **big bad wolf.**" The **little pigs** waved goodbye to their mother and they **trotted** into the woods. They were **laughing** and **smiling** and soon they came across a man who was carrying some **straw.** The **first little pig** said, "may I have some **straw** to build my **house.**" The man said kindly, "Of course, you may." The man gave the **first little pig** some **straw** to build his house. Just before they left the man warned them, "Watch out for the **big bad wolf.**" The **first little pig** built his **house** of **straw.** The **two** other **pigs trotted** on down the road. They were **laughing** and **smiling** and soon they came across a man who was carrying some **sticks.** The **second little pig** said, "May I have some **sticks** to build my **house.**" The man said kindly, "Of course, you may." The man gave the **second** little **pig** some **sticks** to build his house. Just before they left the man warned them, "Watch out for the **big bad wolf.**" The **second little pig** built his **house** of **sticks.** The **third little pig trotted** on down the road. He was laughing and **smiling** and soon he came across a man who was carrying some **bricks.** The third little pig said, "May I have some **bricks** to build my house." The man said kindly, "Of course, you may." The man gave the **third little pig** some **bricks** to build his **house.** Just before they left the man warned him, "Watch out for the **big bad wolf.**"

The **third** little **pig** built his **house** of **bricks.** The **first little pig** had just finished building his **house** of **straw** when the **big bad wolf** appeared. He said, **"Little pig, little pig,** let me come in." The **first little pig** replied, "Not by the hair of my chinny, chin, chin." Then the **wolf** said, Then I'll **huff,** and I'll **puff,** and I will **blow** the **house** down. So, he **huffed,** and he **puffed,** and he **blew** the **house** down. The **first little pig trotted** very quickly to his brother's **house** made of **sticks.** The **second** little **pig** had just finished building his **house** of **sticks** when he heard a knock on the door and to his surprise it was his brother. Suddenly, the **big bad wolf** appeared. He said, **"Little pig, little pig**, let me come in." The **second little pig** replied, "Not by hair of my chinny, chin, chin." Then the **wolf** said, "Then I'll **huff,** and I'll **puff,** and I will **blow** the house down." So, he **huffed,** and he **puffed,** and he **blew** the **house** down. The **two** little **pigs trotted** very quickly to their brother's house made of **bricks**.

The **third little pig** had just finished building his **house** of **bricks** when he heard a knock on the door and to his surprise it was his **two** brothers. Suddenly, the **big bad wolf** appeared. He said, **"Little pig, little pig**, let me come in." The **third** little **pig** replied, "Not by hair of my chinny, chin, chin." Then the **wolf** said, "Then I'll **huff,** and I'll **puff,** and I will **blow** the **house** down." The wolf **huffed,** and he **puffed**. He **huffed,** and he **puffed** but he couldn't **blow** the **house** down. He heard the **three little pigs** inside the **house.** They were **laughing**. This made the **wolf** very angry indeed. He decided he would climb to the top of the roof and come down the chimney. The **third little pig** heard him on the roof and he came up with a clever plan. He put a **big** pot of boiling water on the fire which was just underneath the chimney. The **wolf** came tumbling down the chimney and landed into the **big** pot of boiling water and "SPLASH!" That was the end of the **big bad wolf**. The **three little pigs** lived happily ever after.

THE THREE BILLY GOATS GRUFF

Each child finds a space and sits down. Each child or a group of children are assigned a specific word and a corresponding action. The narrator/teacher reads the story aloud, and when the children hear their word, they must jump up and do their actions. The words are in bold to assist the teacher.

Movement: Action.

Billy goats gruff: Move like a goat and say triplet trip.

Bridge: Two children face each other; they place their arms over their heads and link their fingers together.

Troll: Roar and make an ugly face.

Smallest: Make your body as small as you can.

Middle-sized: Stand up straight.

Bigger/Biggest: Stretch your hands up in the air as high as you can.

Meadow: Get down on your hands and knees and graze on the grass.

Hungry: Rub your tummy.

Brother: Two children link arms.

Brothers: Three children link arms.

Eat: Mime gobbling food.

Narrator: Once upon a time, there lived three **billy goats gruff.** They spent every winter in a barn that kept them nice and warm. But when the summer came, they liked to trippety trip over the **bridge** to the beautiful green **meadow** on the other side of the river. "I'm really **hungry**. I think I will cross the **bridge** to eat some lovely green grass in the **meadow**," said the **smallest billy goat gruff.**

What the **billy goats gruff** didn't know was that under the **bridge**, there lived an ugly **troll**. The **troll** was nasty and horrible.

Nobody crossed the **bridge** without the **troll's** permission, and he never gave permission.

"I can't wait to get to the **meadow**," said the **smallest billy goat gruff.** "Who is that trippety tripping over my **bridge**?" roared the **troll.**

"Oh, it's only me. Please let me pass. I only want to go to the **meadow** to **eat** some sweet grass," pleaded the **smallest billy goat gruff**.

"Oh no, you are not. I'm going to **eat** you," said the **troll.**

"Oh, no, please, Mr. **Troll**, I'm only the **smallest billy goat gruff.** I'm much too tiny for you to **eat**, and I wouldn't taste very good. Why don't you wait for my **brother**, the **middle-sized billy goat gruff?** He is much **bigger** than I am and would be much tastier," said the **smallest billy goat gruff.**

"Well, I suppose I could wait," the **troll** said with a sigh.

"I think I will join my **brother** on the meadow and eat some lovely lush grass," mused the **middle-sized billy goat gruff.**

"Who is that trippety tripping over my **bridge**?" roared the **troll**.

"Oh, it's only me. Please let me pass. I only want to go to the **meadow** to **eat** some sweet grass" said the **middle sized billy goats gruff.**

"Oh no, you are not. I'm going to **eat** you," bellowed the **troll.**

"Oh, no, please, Mr. **Troll**, I'm only the **middle-sized billy goat gruff.** I'm much too tiny for you to **eat,** and I wouldn't taste very good. Why don't you wait for my **brother**, the **biggest billy goat gruff?"** He is much **bigger** than I am and would be much tastier," pleased the **middle-sized billy goat gruff.**

"Well, I suppose I could wait," the **troll** said with a sigh.

"I am alone and hungry. I will join my **brothers** in the **meadow** and get some nice and sweet grass to **eat**," said the **biggest billy goat gruff**.

"Who is that trippety tripping over my **bridge**?" roared the **troll**.

"Oh, it is only me. Please let me pass. I only want to go to the **meadow** to **eat** some sweet grass," said the **biggest billy goat gruff.**

"Oh no, you are not. I'm going to **eat** you," bellowed the **troll**.

"That's what you think!" shouted the **biggest billy goat gruff** angrily. He lowered his horns, galloped along the **bridge** and butted the ugly **troll**. Up, up, up went the **troll** into the air. Then down, down, down into the rushing river below. He disappeared below the swirling waters. "That taught him a lesson," said the **biggest billy goat gruff.** He continued across the **bridge** and met with his **brothers**, and they ate grass and played for the rest of summer.

THE LITTLE RED HEN

Each child finds a space and sits down. Each child or a group of children are assigned a specific word and a corresponding action. The narrator/teacher reads the story aloud, and when the children hear their word, they must jump up and do their actions. The words are in bold to assist the teacher.

Movement: Action.

Little Red Hen: Make yourself as small as possible and cluck around like a chicken.

Plant: Mime digging a hole and planting a seed.

Wheat: Make your body into the shape of a wheat plant.

Dogs: Move and bark like a dog.

Ducks: Waddle and quack like a duck.

Geese: Move like a goose and say "gobble, gobble."

Cats: Move like a cat and meow.

Cut: Use a slashing movement.

Bread and cakes: Mime eating a delicious cake.

Once upon a time, there was a **little red hen** that lived on a farm. She was always busy! She spent all morning laying eggs for the farmer.

"**Little Red Hen**, please lay an egg for my tea," said the farmer. After the **little red hen** had laid her egg, she found a grain of wheat. She wanted to **plant** it in a field.

"I'll ask my animal friends to help me. **Dogs, Dogs**! Will you help me **plant** the **wheat**?" she said.

"Oh no, we will not help you. We are too busy burying our bones. Get the **ducks** to help you," barked the **dogs**.

"**Ducks, Ducks**! Will you help me **plant** the **wheat**?" said the **little red hen.**

"Oh no, we will not help you. We are too busy swimming. Get the **geese** to help you," quacked the **ducks**.

"**Geese, Geese**! Will you help me **plant** the **wheat**?" said the **little red hen.**

"Oh no, we will not help you. We are too busy sunbathing. Get the **cats** to help you," gaggled the **geese**.

"**Cats, Cats**! Will you help me **plant** the **wheat**?" said the **little red hen**.

"Oh no, we will not help you. **Plant** it yourself," meowed the **cats**.

No one would help the **little red hen,** so she **planted** it herself. The sun and the rain helped the **wheat** to grow. Soon, the **wheat** was tall and yellow and needed to be **cut**. "I'll ask my animal friends to help me. **Dogs, Dogs**! Will you help me **cut** the **wheat**?" said the **little red hen.**

"Oh no, we will not help you. We are too busy burying our bones. Get the **ducks** to help you," barked the **dogs**.

"**Ducks, Ducks**! Will you help me **cut** the **wheat**?" said the **little red hen**.

"Oh no, we will not help you. We are too busy swimming. Get the **geese** to help you," **quacked** the **ducks**.

"Geese, Geese! Will you help me cut the wheat?" said the **little red hen**.

"Oh no, we will not help you. We are too busy sunbathing. Get the **cats** to help you," gaggled the **geese**.

"**Cats, Cats**! Will you help me cut the wheat?" said the **little red hen.**

"Oh no, we will not help you. We are too busy washing our faces. **Cut** it yourself," meowed the cats.

So, the **little red hen cut** the **wheat** herself, and she took the **wheat** to the miller. The miller turned the **wheat** into flour.

"Here's your flour to make **bread and cakes**," said the miller.

The **little red hen** thanked the miller. She made **bread and cakes**.

"Who will help me eat the **bread and cakes**?" said the **little red hen**.

"We will!" shouted all the animals.

"Oh no, I will eat it myself. If you want to eat the food, what will you do next time?" asked the **little red hen.**

"We will share the work," said all the animals.

OTHER BOOKS BY THE AUTHOR

Drama Start Series:

Drama Start: Drama Activities, Plays and Monologues for Children (Ages 3-8)

Drama Start Two: Drama Activities for Children (Ages 9-12)

Stage Start: 20 Plays for Children (Ages 3-12)

Stage Start: Two: 20 More Plays for Children (Ages 3-12)

Movement Start: Over 100 Movement Activities and Stories for Children

ESL Drama Start: Drama Activities and Plays for ESL Learners

On Stage Series:

Aesop's Fables on Stage: A Collection of Plays Based on Aesop's Fables

Fairy Tales on Stage: A Collection of Plays for Children

Classics on Stage: A Collection of Plays Based on Classic Children's Stories

Christmas Stories on Stage: A Collection of Plays for Children

Panchatantra on Stage: A Collection of Plays for Children

Hans Christian Andersen's Stories on Stage: A Collection of Plays for Children

Oscar Wilde's Stories on Stage: A Collection of Plays based on Oscar Wilde's Short Stories

Just So Stories on Stage: A Collection of Plays based on Rudyard Kipling's Just So Stories